Folksong

A Ballad of Death, Discovery, and DNA

Cory Goodrich

FINN-PHYLLIS
PRESS

Grateful acknowledgment is made to Terry Smith for permission to reprint an excerpt from "Far Side Banks of Jordan."

Folksong / Cory Goodrich.— 1st ed.

ISBN 978-1-7359743-2-3 (pbk)
ISBN 978-1-7359743-3-0 (eBook)

Book Cover Design by David Barron
Author Photograph by Bari Baskin

www.CoryGoodrich.com
www.FolkSongBook.com

Ghost Girl painting by Cory Goodrich

Pour Mooth (For Mooth)

"Slowly our folk songs grew, part dream and part reality, part past and part present. Each phrase rose from the depths of the heart or was carved out of the rock of experience. Each line was sung smooth by many singers, who tested it against the American reality, until the language became apt and truthful and tough as cured hickory. Here lies the secret to their beauty. They evoke the feeling of a place and of belonging to a particular branch of the human family. They honestly describe or protest against the deepest ills that afflict us—the color bar, our repressed sexuality, our love of violence and our loneliness. Finally, they have been cared for and shaped by so many hands that they have acquired a patina of art, and reflect the tenderest and most creative impulses of the human heart, casting upon our often harsh and melancholy tradition a luster of true beauty."

—*Alan Lomax*

The truth may set you free,
but it may enslave someone else.

They say that there are three sides to every story: yours, mine and the truth. This story is about my connections. Pathways through grief and loss. Rambling country roads that gave me roots and wings. Rivers of music that etched canyons in my psyche.

It is the story about the father who took me in, the father who took me away, and the father who gave me away. It is the story about the woman I knew the least and the woman I knew the most. Is that woman my mother, or me? That is up to you to decide.

If you asked the people around me to tell their account of this tale, you might get a completely different version. Is it any less truthful because the details are different? Maybe. Maybe not.

Memory, like a theatre performance, is ephemeral—there for a shared moment of time and then gone. We shape our memories to fit the narrative we want to tell. Whether the characters in this memoir are villains, heroes, protagonists, or passive observers all depends upon the perspective of the reader.

Is this account factual and true to the past?

Maybe.

Maybe not.

But it is the story as I felt it—as my memories and feelings shaped and directed it.

For the point of this narrative, some memories are combined, some names have been changed, and some details are probably only true to my childhood self. But this account is as brutally honest as I can make it, because above all, the truth is imperative.

No more pretty lies.

PROLOGUE

*If a family tree falls in the woods and no one
is around to see it, do I even exist?*

He wants me to write the story of her life. When I suggest he do it, since she told him all the secrets she wouldn't tell me, my stepfather refuses. He has already written the story of his father, and of his father's father, so it is my duty to write the story of my mother. Maybe he wants me to understand her, to discover what drove her to the choices that ruined me. Or maybe he needs me to explain her mysteries to him. But in the fifty-one years I knew her before her death, my mother ran from the truth. Does she want her life dissected now, after she is gone, or does she want to disappear with the wind, like her ashes blown into the Santa Rita mountains, to float gently off into distant memory?

I can't tell her story.

But I can tell mine.

You gotta walk that lonesome valley
You gotta walk it by yourself.
Ain't nobody here can walk it for you
You gotta walk that lonesome valley by yourself.

My mamma said when she was dying
Just before she's going on,
Lord I'm just going over Jordan.
I'm just goin' over home.

My daddy said when he lay dying
Just before his breath was gone,
My darling child just trust in Jesus
And he will surely lead us home.

—traditional

PART I

HEART SONGS

CHAPTER ONE

THE BEGINNING

T he last day that I felt joy—real, soul-bubbling-over joy—was October 3, 2017, the day before my mother's open-heart surgery.

I had driven to a quirky little folk instrument store in Tucson, aptly named The Folk Shop. It was my first taste of solitude in over a week, and I needed the respite before the coming storm. I found in this store my people: people who love autoharps and ukuleles and mandolins and a Finnish harp called a kantele that, in retrospect, I wish I had purchased. By the time I would return to that store, on Friday the Thirteenth no less, the harp would be gone, right along with every scrap of knowing who I was. My surety of self would have vanished, leaving me with nothing but an echo of a tune I remembered faintly but couldn't quite grasp; the words and the melody ephemeral, just on the tip of my tongue, frustratingly out of reach.

Though you would never know it from the bubbly persona I show the world as a stage performer and singer-songwriter, the truth is, I have always felt different, a little isolated, the one at the party who observes the fun but can't quite join in because of this irrational, internal fear of not belonging. Ah, the joys of social anxiety, my constant companion. I have always been saddled with that most unwelcome friend, curiously anxious in all the areas of my life that mattered most—in my career, with my friends, and especially with my family growing up. The one place I have always been able to be my undiluted self is with the family unit I created: with my daughters, Celia and Genevieve, and my husband, David. But even there, in my most secure place, I sometimes deliberately hold myself separate and apart, afraid that one day the shoe won't fit, and Cinderella will be strong-armed out of the ball for being an imposter and stealing the glass slippers.

Like a Steven Spielberg film, my life has been under-scored with longing. I have a vivid memory of my younger self in my elementary school years, sitting backwards on the nubby, cornflower blue couch in front of the picture window in our house in Delaware. I looked through that window up to the stars and felt the incomprehensible vastness of the Universe. I wondered how someone so small could feel connected with something—someone—she'd never met. Was HE looking up at the very same stars? In those younger years, I didn't know who HE was, but I felt his absence like an emptiness in my stomach. Like hunger. I would whisper to no one, "Where are you?" I thought maybe I was looking for a lover, my other half...someone who looked like Speed Racer or sounded like Bobby Darin. But I wonder now if the man I was looking for, begging, *Please come find me,* was my father. Maybe it was my brother. But now it is too late for one, and I am too vulnerable and broken for the other.

And the moon looks down on this sleepy town and I wonder,
Do the stars shine bright where you are tonight? I wonder.
Will I find you? Will I ever find you?

And so, on that October day in a musty and crowded storefront in Tucson, Arizona, I found a comforting connection with this strange obsession of mine: folk music. I've long found solace in the thought that these folk songs have been carried across the ocean, from Ireland and Scotland and Africa, to come to this strange new world. Every piece of music we know, no matter how original we think it may be, has roots that stretch back to our forefathers, wandering the moors and singing plaintive tunes to stave away fear and boredom and hunger. The singers longed for women they could not have, for men lost to war or adventure, and for mothers who died whispering their child's name, saying, "Come home to me, my darling."

This music touches me. I don't know why, but these old story songs have always resonated deeply within me. I hear ghost balladeers crooning their legacy to the wind. Remember, remember. They haunt me as keenly as do the ghosts of my own past, day-in, day-out.

I play a fair number of different instruments, though none proficiently. Autoharp, guitar, ukulele, accordion, piano, dulcimer, even the musical saw. So, finding this quirky little store the day before my mother's surgery was a gift; a little bit of peace and a reminder that some things do carry on for eternity. Music is a legacy that underscores our lives and drifts over oceans of time to our children and their children's children. The songs our hearts sing are the loudest—and the most persistent.

My mother had decided to have open-heart surgery, a horrifying proposition for an eighty-nine-year-old woman weakened from lung cancer and leaky valves. Or, at least, it was horrifying for her youngest daughter. I dreaded it. I knew from the moment she called to tell me of her necessity for this surgery that this was it: she was going to die. Realistically, I knew that, at eighty-nine, that day was coming soon anyway, but this was clearly not the ending I would have chosen for her. I feared she would never recover from the violent aftermath of having her chest split in two. I knew that she was not-so-secretly preparing to leave this mortal coil. That she was done. That something she would never speak of had broken her heart so thoroughly that no surgeon could repair it. I begged her to reconsider, but there was no swaying my mother. When she made up her mind to do something, by God, she did it. She would not simply fade away, she would go out in a flourish, with all eyes upon her. In the end, she would die just as she lived.

And when she died, neither one of us had any idea she would become the hero of my story. That "The Ballad of Ernie and Don" would become my underscored motif.

Ernie and her father, Caleb Eslinger

CHAPTER TWO

ROOTS

O n October 21, 1927, Caleb Eslinger was asked to make an impossible choice. Nettie Eslinger screamed and panted in her bedroom, unsuccessfully struggling to push her first child from the womb. The midwife feared they would lose both mother and child if swift action weren't taken, so the doctor was called. After checking Nettie's status, he pulled her husband Caleb into the hallway and demanded an answer to the fateful question: "If I can save only one, who's life should I choose?"

What ran through Caleb's mind in that moment? How do you choose between the woman you love and the innocent child you will grow to adore? How do you prioritize the giver of life over the life itself, one whom you already know intimately over the one to whom you gave the spark of life—your flesh, your legacy?

Apparently, it wasn't such an impossible decision after all, because without hesitation, Caleb answered, "The mother. Save Nettie."

Fortunately, the doctor was never required to act on this Sophie's Choice kind of decision. My mother, Ernestine, finally emerged from the womb in which she was lodged, as stubborn in birth as she was in later life. She gave her mama hell from the start.

My mother never gave a medical explanation for her complicated and traumatic birth. That wasn't the point of her narrative. The reason for the choice between mother and child wasn't important. The significance of this event was subconsciously layered into the story Nettie oft repeated to her daughter, sealing their doomed relationship and establishing their order of importance in the family.

When Nettie spoke of her daughter Ernestine's birth, she told her: When your father had to choose between us, he chose me. The "over you" was overtly implied.

Your father loved me more.

As harsh as Caleb's decision may seem, especially from my perspective as his grandchild, knowing that my very existence potentially rested upon the outcome of that choice, I have sympathy for his desperate reply to the doctor. He was an ardent young man madly in love with his new bride, Antoinette ("Nettie")—a man who had yet to know paternal devotion and who could not fathom just how precious this new life would be or how he could care for a newborn child alone—a single father in the days when such a role simply did not exist. What I don't understand is why Nettie felt the need to hammer this story into her daughter's psyche.

What void did my grandmother long to fill that caused her to so desperately need to show proof of her own worth? To invalidate my mother's existence and her father's love? What sort of deep-seated insecurity did she instill in Ernestine? My mother's father was forced to declare his loyalty. My mother would not allow my father to make the same choice. So she took us both out of the equation.

Nettie and Ernie

My nana, Antoinette Eslinger, was by all accounts a real-life Mama Rose, a starstruck stage mother with lofty aspirations for her three daughters. She was intelligent and wildly determined, and when her own attempts at a music career stalled, she married handsome Caleb Eslinger, a young accountant who by strange coincidence shared her birthday, June 6, 1899. Caleb had just accepted an accounting job across the country in California and was preparing to relocate when he met Antoinette Marie Solia. He fell so hard for pretty Nettie, as she was nicknamed, that he turned down the West Coast job in order to stay in Wilmington and start a family.

After Ernestine was born, two other daughters, Joanne and Eileen, soon followed. The three girls were given ballet, piano, guitar, and voice lessons, and when Nettie discovered her young daughters could sing in perfect three-part harmony, she turned her sharp eye toward the potential careers for her attractive and talented girls. It was the era of the Andrew Sisters, and copycat groups were in high demand. During the Great Depression and the war years that followed, the Stairstep Sisters, as Antoinette's daughters were named, gained a modest amount of fame and success. They performed at the 1939 World's Fair and on the Major Bowe's National Amateur Hour Radio Program, for the Red Cross and the USO, from Philadelphia to New York City and all points in between. I see pictures of my mother in her stage costumes, singing with her sisters, and she looks elated, smiling, and in her element. A born performer.

Ernestine, Joanne, and Eileen

Ernestine, Eileen, and Joanne

But the truth is, my mother hated every second of her stage career, and she hated her mother as well.

"It was terrible, all the constant music lessons. I didn't have a lot of time for school activities, we were always marched off to performances. My mother ruined my life."

My mother ruined my life.

Ernestine complained bitterly throughout the years of all the events and experiences she was forced to miss in order to act as a performing monkey: school dances and social events, dating, and a normal teenage life. Her talented sisters loved the music and dance lessons, and they loved the glamour and excitement of performing, but rebellious Ernie did not. Eventually, to escape her mother's control—and maybe even to thumb her nose at Nettie's aspirations of stardom for the Stairstep Sisters—Ernestine married a boy who lived down the street. The tall, impossibly lanky Tommy Hyatt. She was just twenty years old. It was an ill-fated union. Tommy Hyatt was irresponsible and had no ambition—something Ernie clearly had, but a thing no woman was encouraged to nurture in those days.

My mother rarely spoke of this escape marriage. The only detail she ever shared with me about the four and a half years she was married to her first husband was that Tommy Hyatt's father purchased a drug store for his son to manage, but Tommy never wanted to work. He would refuse to show up in the mornings to open the store. His indolence drove my mother crazy. When he complained about having to take public transit, Ernie bought him a brand-new car with the money she had earned as a secretary. When she finally had enough of his laziness, she told him to keep the car she had paid for in exchange for a tidy divorce. When my mother was done with something, she was done. Now, the fact that she was enamored of a tall, blond co-worker may have contributed to this hasty marital exit, but she never admitted to that.

Rather than become a singer as my nana wanted, or a secretary or a wife like society wanted, my mother longed to study archaeology. But, by the time she was ready for college, her father was dead from acute pancreatitis, and widowed Nettie did not have the money to pay for her daughter's further education. Ernie shifted her aspirations to becoming a flight attendant—a stewardess as they were called in her day—because they were lucky enough to get paid to travel the world, and, as she said, they always looked so smart and elegant in their uniforms. It's no surprise to me that my mother would long for a vocation solely for the costume. Appearances always played an important role in her life.

Unfortunately, in those days, airline stewardesses were also required to be nurses, and playing the part of caretaker and healer was simply not something that interested Ernie. She settled for a secretarial position with Hercules Inc., a chemical company in Wilmington. Because she was clever and very beautiful, and had a good working knowledge of chemistry, she was highly sought after—especially by my future father, the tall and handsome almost-Olympian Tom Goodrich. The fact that she was legally, at the time, Ernestine Hyatt, did not deter either of them.

But what did Ernestine really want for herself? In many early morning phone conversations with my mother while I was concurrently raising my children and pursuing a career in the theatre, she wistfully told me how lucky I was not only to have a dream but to be able to follow it. She could not overstate how fortunate I was to have a husband who allowed me to follow my ambitions and supported my unstable career as an actress and singer. I rolled my eyes and tried to ignore the blatant and ingrained sexism inherent in her generation (I failed), but it made me wonder, What dreams did my mother have? What would she have pursued if she had been given a chance to become who and what she wanted to become? Not what her mother wanted her to be, and not who three (ultimately) husbands and four children needed her to be.

Sadly, I cannot ask her. I should have asked her during one of those phone calls, but at the time I was too consumed with my own dreams and failures. And, let's face it, she probably wouldn't have told me anyway. She zealously guarded and protected her past, especially from the ones who loved her most.

Why don't we ask these kinds of questions before it is too late? Why don't we realize how vital it is to paint the full picture of the ones we love before they are gone? Why do we see our parents only as parents, not as fully realized and complicated people with hopes and heartbreaks and secrets? As lovers and friends and children with hurts that need to be healed?

Maybe we can't ever know the whole of a person. Maybe we need to divide them into categories or chapters or archetypes so that they can play their respective roles in our own soap operas. Now that I know a bit of the truth about the part I played in my mother's drama, I feel like I know her more...and also less...than I ever thought I did.

CHAPTER THREE

THE ACTRESS

If I were to give you the brief rundown of my life—write my own eulogy, so to speak—I'd tell you that I, Corinne Marie Goodrich, was born in Wilmington, Delaware on September 30th, 1966. When I made my earthly debut, my mother's obstetrician reportedly said, "Well, Ernie, you finally got one that looks like you." This oft repeated narrative was echoed constantly by my mother and my aunts, as if they were trying to etch it deeply into my brain. *You look like your mother.* I certainly didn't look like my blond father and the rest of my siblings.

In 1974, a month before my eighth birthday, when Tom and Ernie divorced and my mother married Jim Perkins before the ink had dried on her divorce papers, we moved to Clarkston, Michigan. The next ten years were fractured. I spent the school year in Michigan with Ernie and Jim, and the hot languid summers in Delaware with my father (Tom), and later with my pseudo evil step-monster, Anita. Anita had bleached blond hair and big boobs and the innate ability to make anyone feel inadequate, but she also introduced me to the Broadway recording of the musical *Evita*, which instantly changed my life.

I fell in love with the theatre and the immediate family it created while I was in high school. God knows I desperately needed that sense of belonging. Being shuttled between two homes left me feeling like I fully belonged to neither. My high school drama teacher, Barb Gibson, or "Ma" as we called her, recognized that displaced longing in me, and she saw a seed of talent that was waiting to bloom. She became my mentor and my biggest advocate, and I did anything I could to please her, including choosing her Alma Mater, Michigan State University, as my own.

After graduating with a somewhat useless BFA in musical theatre, I moved to Chicago, where I have worked as an actress/singer/musician/songwriter/painter/mother/ record producer/recording artist and general all-around creative whirling dervish for the past thirty years. To look at me, you'd see a woman living in the suburbs with a thriving career, two intelligent and happy daughters, and a supportive husband, two cats, a dog, and a lizard. I've done commercials with Marie Osmond for Nutrisystem, been on a handful of TV shows, produced seven Christmas CDs for charity, and won several acting and music awards. Oh, and I'm blond. On paper, I'm picture perfect.

But if you peel back that always-smiling Midwestern veneer, you'll see someone much different. I'm currently in the midst of an identity crisis of epic proportions. I have horrible bouts of anxiety and depression; I'm angry most of the time and suicidal some of the time. I question who I am and why I am in this soul-sucking business, and why I have made some of the more questionable choices I have made in my life. I come from a broken home, had a barely present father, battled with my mother and stepfather, am a constant attention seeker, and became an actor because I didn't get enough love in my childhood. I'm also not a real blond. Whatever.

Listen, I know that in the grand scheme of things, I'm pretty lucky. I'm not going to try to convince you that my life was horrible and beg you to pity poor little sad Cory. I know that I wasn't raised in poverty; my life wasn't in danger every time I walked to school. I haven't gone to jail or been addicted to heroin or sold my body to pay for losses at the casino. I'm just a plain, ordinary woman who has suffered some life-altering revelations but has, at least so far, survived.

Within these pages, I'm telling you this ridiculously personal story so that you will not feel you are alone, the way I have always felt alone. I'm telling you this story because, like many in her generation, my mother was stingy with the details of her life. She shared so few of her stories with me, or with any of her children. She attempted to erase her past, or maybe she was just trying to earnestly guard it. She left too many words unspoken and story chapters untold. So, in honor of my mother (or perhaps more accurately, to rebel against her secret-keeping) and most definitely to what would be her complete horror were she still alive, I'm going to share all of mine with you, because in spite of growing up in the shadow of half-told truths and secrets, I am determined to find some way to live out loud.

Okay, I'll share *most* of my secrets.

Will you settle for *some?*

The only way out is through.

So let's go.

CHAPTER FOUR

SNAPSHOTS

I am spending the week before my mother's surgery at her home in Green Valley, Arizona. It is a beautiful house, open, airy and white, and it's peppered with Native American art and jewelry. In the transom windows, a parade of Kachina dolls cast shadows of dancing medicine men across the high walls of her dining room in the late afternoon sun.

Mama has always taken such pleasure in the shadow dance of the dolls; it was her brilliant idea to place them up in the windows to catch the sun that allowed them to ghost walk across her walls during their daily ceremony of praise. Native American spiritual beliefs hold that a Kachina is an immortal being who acts as a messenger between the human and spirit worlds. I like thinking that maybe my mother has become the messenger between the spirit world and mine, whispering secrets in my ear as I sit writing and drinking coffee in the early morning quiet. Is she making her dance across the Western skies now? Is she finally free to pursue her dreams in spirit form?

My birthday party, September 30th, 2017,
four days before Mama's surgery.

The Kachina Dolls, Green Valley Arizona

Ernestine Eslinger

In the bedroom closet of that house is a carefully curated box my mother left behind when she died. A yellow
cardboard box full of photographs, newspaper clippings,
and scrapbooks that serve as a summation of the entirety of
her life—a life that I knew nothing about. That old Greek
myth got the story wrong; Pandora's box had nothing on
Ernestine's.

My mother was what they used to call a Looker. She
was incandescent. I had no idea how beautiful she had been
when she was young. Not until I later opened this box of
memories after her death and discovered photos of her as a
child, teenager, and young married woman would I see the

spark and vivacity of Early Ernestine. The way she smiled at the camera as if she had a secret or was captured in the midst of a full throttle laugh, uninhibited and open, a laugh I rarely got to hear. By the time I became less self-absorbed and able to see her as something besides my mother, she was frosting her hair and battling the spreading middle that so often comes with menopause and depression. It's not that she wasn't still beautiful in her mid and old age—she certainly was. Her skin was flawless and unlined, and she always appeared at least ten years younger than her actual age. But some kind of wall had been erected: a glass wall through which you could see her beauty but couldn't feel the full warmth of her light.

She went through so many incarnations in her lifetime: performer "Tine"—first as a member of the Stairstep Sisters, which was later renamed The Debs of Rhythm—who took a million pre-selfie pictures in a bathing suit, romping with her high school friends, fully prescient of her great figure and captivating smile; rebellious bride who married to escape her mother's control; a working woman attending company cocktail parties at the Hercules Country Club, surrounded by men and capturing the eye of the camera above her; Ernestine Hyatt, standing between her current husband, Tommy, and her future husband, Tom; Ernie Goodrich, pregnant, holding new babies—Thomas Jr. and Susie and Dale—and eventually a baby who looked more like her than the others; darker, hazel-eyed, round; Erni Perkins, (now intentionally spelled without the final 'e') square dancer, whip smart bridge partner, and world traveler.

A party at Hercules. Ernie, with her mother Antoinette

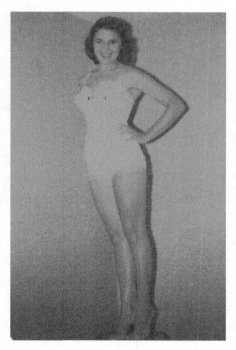

Ernestine, the bathing beauty

Tommy, Dale, Ernie, and Susie, before I was born.

Ernie, between husbands—
Tom Goodrich (future) & Tommy Hyatt (current)

Within the large yellow cardboard box is a smaller Wanamaker's gift box labelled "Cory" with my mother's small, spikey handwriting. This box holds close to a hundred Polaroids of me as a child dressed in elaborate costumes that my mother created: The Flying Nun, a witch, a cowgirl

wearing boots with two cap gun pistols in a holster, Raggedy
Ann with homemade yarn wig and white starched pinafore. It
really is no wonder I became an actress. My mother groomed
me for the theatre by dressing me up in all those beautiful
hand-built costumes. I learned at a very early age that
becoming someone else was much preferable to being me.

Then, there is a period completely devoid of pictures.
Around 1972, when I turned six, the pictures stop.

Where is Ernie during these years? Where am I?

The photographic record of her life begins again after my graduation from high school. There are a million photos of her world travels with my stepfather, Jim, during the time when she morphed into Erni Perkins, dropping the final "e" from her name seemingly out of the blue. Once, when I addressed a letter to "Ernie Perkins," she was petulant, accusing me of not knowing how to spell her name. I was confused. When did that happen? Was there an announcement? An E-dropping ceremony? There were a thousand hurts I was supposed to see and understand in her that I never did or could. She wore her resentment like a scarf, tied tightly around her neck, keeping her from speaking out.

The official story of the missing E goes like this: After retiring to Arizona, Mama and Jim purchased a golf cart with which they would slowly traverse the geriatric paved streets of Green Valley. This golf cart was monogrammed "Jim and Ernie" on the driver's side panel. For some reason, strangers consistently addressed Jim as Ernie, and he became irritated at having to constantly correct them. So, in order to prevent the gender misnomer, he demanded she adopt a more feminine spelling of her name. At sixty-five years of age, Mama changed her name. Ernestine Emma Eileen Eslinger Hyatt Goodrich Perkins altered her name once again, and morphed into yet another version of who she was supposed to be based on someone else's demands.

I had such a visceral response when she told me of her requisite name change. It made me furious, triggering some (justified) feminist rebellion in me. It still makes me sad and determined to be me, regardless of what I am named, whether Cory Goodrich, Cory Barron, or Cory Garnett.

The infamous golf cart, post 'e' removal.

When I married David Barron in 1990, I flat-out refused to take his last name. His traditional family interpreted my determined gesture as a sign that I was not fully committed to the marriage; that I was too loud and outspoken (I am) and perhaps too filled with a sense of self to be a true partner (I'm not). I railed back that Goodrich was my father's name, and it was therefore my name, and I had no intention of becoming someone else for any man. Goodrich was my legacy.

Which is ironic, because that name should not be mine.

My father Tom's mother, Harriet Goodrich, married Harry Ervin Popejoy on May 2nd, 1906. Harry and Harriet—just saying the two names together pleases my sense of the absurd. After fathering five boys, restless Harry decided that he no longer liked the life he was living, and he took off to follow a redhead, abandoning poor Harriet and her young children. Eventually, Harry married the redhead without obtaining a legal divorce (and later died of syphilis, a point

I raise to illustrate karma's wicked sense of humor). Harriet, enraged and forsaken, moved home with her brother and reclaimed her family name: Goodrich. Bold for a woman in the 1920s. I admire the act of protest.

This shift left her sons conflicted. Which name should they use? To whom would they declare their familial loyalty? Wendell and Bruce retained their father's name, Popejoy, and my father and his brothers, Joe and Grant, adopted their mother's nom de guerre, Goodrich. Grant drowned in Lake Michigan at the age of fifteen, which left only Joe and my father to carry on the Goodrich family name. I would take up that banner as well, proudly claiming my defiant grandmother's maiden name.

Which begs the question: What is the significance of a name? Is Goodrich who I am? Does my choice to keep this name define me? And, if this mantle that I have claimed as my birthright is all a lie, does that make me a lie? Am I a joke for doggedly holding onto one name when Mama had a million different titles and personalities, and slid between them as easily as a chameleon changes his colors?

These are the questions that plague me: Who am I? Should I carry on the Goodrich name? Does the father who raised me (and, subsequently, his last name) define my identity?

Because...what if that last name has been wrong all along, and no one bothered to tell me?

CHAPTER FIVE

QUESTION MARKS

I n mid-September when my mother called to say that her surgery was scheduled and ask would I please come out to Arizona to help her through the procedure and the rehab that would follow, I froze. I literally couldn't speak a word on the other end of the line except for an extremely eloquent, "Okay." Then, there was a seemingly endless silence. Unspoken words hovered in the air between us until I blurted out a frantic, "Don't you dare die on my birthday." File this under the "Things you say that totally make you feel like an ass and you wish you could take back" column. That column is so very long.

I hung up the phone, and my heart started racing and my hands shaking. It was a feeling I'd get pretty accustomed to over the next month. I booked a flight, rearranged work schedules, and conferred with my siblings on the best way to coordinate our visits. Mama would have surgery on September 29th, and my brother Dale would stay from September 27th to October 3rd. I would stay until the 7th, when I promised to be home for my daughter's Homecoming dance. Susie would come in on the 5th while Mama was still in the hospital, and would be there to supervise her transfer to the rehabilitation center. I planned to come back to Arizona and resume Mama-care on the 17th. No one ever knew what the hell Tommy would do, so we didn't figure him into the equation.

But, as we are all painfully aware, things never go as planned. After my flight was booked (as a non-refundable fare because I am cheap), my mom's surgery was rescheduled to October 4th, which meant Dale and I would be in Arizona for a full week prior to her procedure with no real purpose other than to spend time with her, ensure she was building strength for the surgery, and calm her anxiety—while most definitely not burdening her with our own.

It's a careful dance you do, dealing with someone who is about to have major surgery. On one hand, you know that Death is just waiting there in the room, patiently watching to see if this is His time to move in. You recognize the possibility of Death, and you feel His icy presence there, but you don't want to acknowledge the son of a bitch. If you actually say, "Hey, Mama, what are those things that you've always wanted to tell us but haven't been able to until now? Have you told everyone you loved them? Have you shared your secrets, because you may not have the chance to do so ever again?" If you say those things, do you open the door to the reality that disaster could happen? By acknowledging that Death is possible, do you inadvertently invite Him in? Or, do you bravely and falsely turn a blind eye to the specter in the corner of the room, hoping He will become weary of being ignored and go someplace He is feared and respected? Instead, you say, "Let's pack your bags now for the rehab center." You say, "No, don't tell me who gets what jewelry, you'll be able to figure that out later." You don't say, "Tell me the stories now, just in case you don't make it through."

And that is foolish. Because now, I wish to God that I had asked the questions. I wish I'd had the hard conversations that my mother and I danced around my entire life. I wish I had said, "Tell me the story because you may not have the chance to tell me ever again. I deserve to no longer feel like a question mark."

But I didn't have that courage.

I was afraid of the answer.

CHAPTER SIX

CAGED

During the summer of 1974, things were in upheaval at our house in Delaware. Mama and Daddy had been fighting. Brutal arguments. My mother was locked out of the house, and I'd scream for her, my chubby hands pressed up against the screen door, while my father threatened to "tell the truth about Cory." My siblings called a family conference down in the basement by the old wooden toy box to explain to seven-year-old me that I would be moving with my mother and Dale to Michigan, while Susie and Tommy remained in Delaware with Daddy. The three of them showed me the big map of the United States that hung above the toy box (inside of which I was often found eating white bread and Miracle Whip sandwiches, pretending I was living secluded in a submarine).

At seven, I had no real comprehension of where Delaware was, let alone this foreign country named Michigan, shaped like a mitten in the middle of the map. It appeared to be only a few inches away from Delaware, so why was everyone so upset? There was a solemnity about that meeting that was unsettling. No one knew what to say. After the meeting was over, I climbed into the wooden box, pulled the lid shut, and sat in darkness, confused about what was coming next.

What came next was a divorce, a wedding we weren't invited to, and Mama leaving for her honeymoon while I had my tonsils removed. I recovered from this surgery in my parents' king-sized bed with no mother to comfort me. She was in Niagara Falls with her new husband, Jim, while her child cried her own waterfall of tears. Mrs. Alouise, my father's "special friend," took care of me and gifted me a book to pass the time while I was recovering. The book was *Edith and Mr. Bear,* the story of a doll who lives with Mr. Teddy Bear and his son, Little Bear. Edith feels that she does not belong because she is a naughty doll, while the Teddy bears are kind and well-behaved. I felt like Edith.

And then, one day, Mama returned with her new husband while Daddy was at work. Jim was trim and short and looked like Buck Owens from "Hee-Haw." My father, Tom, was tall and handsome and made me feel like he could lift me up to the stars. Jim was none of those things.

Seven-year-old me shyly showed Jim my prized possessions: three stuffed animal kittens my sister Susie had hand-sewn for my birthday. Their names were Johnny, Frederic, and Crystal. Crystal had long eyelashes and gemstone eyes and was a perfectly appropriate girlish pink. Johnny, Crystal's brother, was a cornflower blue cat that played jazz music. But Frederic, named for composer Frederic Chopin, was pale yellow, and he was my favorite. He was a classical musician cat, and, as the real Chopin was tortured for love of George Sand, Frederic was tortured with love for the otherwise indifferent, long-lashed, and endlessly flirtatious

Crystal. The three little stuffed kittens lived together in a wicker breadbasket, and I loved them. So, when I was introduced to my new stepfather, Jim, I naturally introduced him to my cherished pets, and he did what any engineer trying to impress his new stepdaughter would do...he designed and built an impromptu cage made out of a shoebox with drinking straws inset as bars.

To seven-year-old me, this was horrifying. Why on earth would he put my prized, musical, and most gentle kitten friends in a cage? I could relate to their panic at being locked behind bars. It was how I felt. Trapped.

Later that evening, Jim kissed my mother in the living room of my father's house, and I wanted to sink into the floor. I didn't know why it made me uncomfortable, but I looked over at Dale to see what to do, and he looked ashen. He wouldn't look at me, and I knew he wanted to sink into the floor too. This was our new reality. Daddy would stay in Delaware, and we would climb into the moving van with Mama and the man who kissed her under my father's roof, and watch through the side view mirror as our life got smaller and farther away.

My mother has always been a conundrum to me. Whether or not it was true, I often felt invisible to her. Maybe it was because I was the last of four children, born when she was in her late thirties with a seven-year gap between me and my closest brother, Dale. Maybe it was because I was the catalyst of a drama that would eventually lead to her divorce and the uprooting of her/our whole world. Maybe she felt like it was her turn to live her own life again after years of child rearing and husband taming.

Throughout my early childhood, Ernie was frequently absent, or at least that is how I remember it. My sister Susie was forced to devise creative tricks in order to quell my frequent Missing-Mama panic attacks: magic sugar-water potions to stop the tears, milk and blue food coloring elixirs that would imbue me with bravery and the courage to endure the separation. Susie, eleven years my senior, was really more of a mother to me than Ernie with an "e."

After The Divorce, life for Mama became a whirlwind of honeymooning, house-hunting, and establishing a new life in Michigan with Jim, Dale and myself. There were tears and homesickness and an overwhelming sense of displacement for all of us—mother and daughter and son alike. Then, after I graduated from college and moved to Chicago, there was another whirlwind of upheaval for her, another new life, this time in Arizona. This meant more house hunting and displacement and rebuilding of community. And from there, she travelled all over the world, engaged in anything at all to keep her thoughts and memories at bay. But when time and age finally slowed her down enough to allow her time to evaluate the course of her life, the bitterness crept in along with the panic that came from the realization that maybe she didn't like the choices she had made or the man she had last married. Her final years were steeped in resentment for her mother (who, remember, she claimed had ruined her life) and for Jim, the man she married to rescue her from Delaware and my father, Tom. It's possible that those years were steeped in resentment for someone else, too, but I am only guessing.

Ernie married Edward James Perkins (Jim) in August of 1974, shortly after her divorce from Tom Goodrich was finalized. Jim worked for Chrysler in Detroit and was, himself, recently divorced from his wife, Hortense, who understandably went by the name June. Jim and June had four children of their own.

Jim's two youngest boys spent the weekend at our new house in Michigan maybe twice during our first year there. Eventually, they stopped coming over at all and cut their father out of their lives completely. I didn't know if this was his fault or his ex-wife's fault or my mother's fault, but I figured Ernie just didn't want to have anything to do with them.

Honestly, I didn't think about my new step-siblings much at all while I was growing up in that silent, tense household. I was struggling to find my own way out, and it never occurred to me that maybe Jim's children were struggling to find a way in. I never wondered where they were or if it bothered Jim not to see them. I just assumed Mama didn't want them there, so they stayed away. I understood all too well what it felt like to be an unwelcome visitor because I was that unwelcome visitor in the eyes of Daddy's new live-in girlfriend, Anita, any time I was back in Delaware. Because of this understanding, I judged my mother harshly for not welcoming Chris, Eddie, Kathy, and Reed Perkins into our lives with open arms. But, as it turned out, I was wrong about her and her decisions, just as I was wrong about so many other things.

In that week before her surgery, Erni wandered around her white house in her white nightgown, white socks, and white hair, muttering to me the things that bothered her most. "Jim wouldn't go to Kathy when she was dying. How can I forgive him for that?" She was finally questioning what kind of man she had married, something I had questioned from the very day I met him.

CHAPTER SEVEN

THE SILVER WATCH

September 27, 2017—Green Valley, Arizona

Jim and I pulled up to the house in the Chrysler 300. He had just picked me up at the Tucson airport, and the forty-five-minute drive to Green Valley was tense and quiet as usual, but at least this time we had something concrete to discuss: my mother's health.

Jim described the litany of doctor visits and diagnoses that had led to the decision to cut my mother's chest open to repair two leaky valves and atrial fibrillation. He spoke of her refusal to live a second longer in this condition—weakened and tethered to her oxygen lifeline. He hoped that my visit would calm her agitation. I hoped it would too, but I wished there were something to calm my own.

As we pulled into the driveway, Mama came to the front door. I always feel a mixture of terror and anxiety leading up to seeing an aging parent after a long period. It's the same nervousness I felt every summer on the car ride back to Delaware and Daddy. The overwhelming fear of seeing how much he had deteriorated, and hoping to be relieved instead to see how much he hadn't. I girded myself this time with my ailing mother, prepared to see the worst, and I was grateful to see that she wasn't nearly as broken as I had anticipated. Yes, Erni was pale, and the skin that had always garnered so many compliments was hanging loosely off of her frame from rapid weight loss. She had an oxygen tube in her nose and its long tail followed her throughout the house, but she was smartly dressed in her preferred white... always white...and she had just returned from the salon, so her hair and nails were freshly done. She wore bright pink lipstick and, of course, her jewelry.

This was one thing I could always count on: my mother would be wearing jewelry. Even as she toddled through the house in the last week before her surgery, she wore her black opal ring from Australia—the one I am now wearing on my left hand, her opal bracelet with the silver "family" charm, and her sterling silver Silpada watch. I bought her that watch years back with my consultant's discount. She loved it. Jim complained that he bought her an expensive Seiko watch with diamonds on the face, and when it died, rather than replacing the piece that had broken, she had the watch melted down for the gold. It bothered him that she wore a cheap silver watch instead, and I didn't tell him she had gotten it from me. I also didn't mention that I knew just how much she loved that watch. She told me on every visit. It was symbolic of her choosing me over Jim. Echoes of Caleb's Choice, like ripples in the pond of time. History repeating itself.

My mother chose me.

That watch went missing after her death, and I still

wonder if the trophy was conveniently misplaced because it was a sign of her loyalty. I search for it every time I return to Arizona, under the bed, in her closet, inside a pocket of her purse. It has vanished.

As I climbed from the passenger side of the red Chrysler, Mama came to the front door, and the first words out of her mouth were, "Come here, I want to give you your birthday present."

"Mama, I can wait, my birthday is only three days away."

"No, I'm giving it to you now." She clearly had an agenda, and she was determined to stick to it.

"It's not new," she said apologetically, and handed me a small grey box. Inside the box was a vintage opal bracelet. I am very familiar with my mother's jewelry and yet I had never seen this particular piece. We used to spend hours going over her collection as she recalled the story of where and when each piece was purchased, how much it cost, and why she loved it. Why had I never seen this bracelet before?

An intricately woven gold bangle with seven opals (her birthstone) in a cluster on the top, it was beautiful and unique, and of course I loved it, as she knew I would. I asked her to tell me the story behind its acquisition, and she was oddly vague. "Marge and I got it before you were born. Someone told us about a place in New Jersey that sold jewelry, and I bought it for about a hundred dollars, then."

I don't know if that story is completely true, as I am now second guessing all of my mother's stories and convenient omissions, but there was an urgency behind her giving me this gift. I have my suspicions why, but I guess I will never know the truth because she died with that secret also locked up in her broken heart. Maybe she did buy it for herself, or perhaps it was actually given to her as a gift. And if so, by whom? Why had I never seen it before? Why was it so important that she give it to me before she had her surgery? Another litany of questions to add to my ever-growing list.

Mama then handed me a book, *The House at Riverton*. "You have to read this. It has a surprise ending and I think you'll love it. It's important that you read this." It wasn't the type of book she usually read. My mother loved Michener and history books, not upstairs/downstairs bodice rippers. But I noted her insistence and promised to read it. I carried the book with me to the hospital during her stay, but I could never focus long enough to get past the first page.

Next, Mama brought me into the den to show me the specific personal items I was to distribute in the event she did not survive the operation. I tried to listen and make mental notes, but I didn't want to appear overly eager or let her think that I believed she was going to die. The fact that I even felt that ominous sensation made me try to hide it even more. There were a million details I wanted to know, but I would deny myself the questions in an effort to prove to her my confidence that she would be fine. Yet, I didn't really believe that, and she knew it.

I can hide exactly zero emotions. It's what makes me a good actress, I suppose. You can read my thoughts like a book in large print. It frustrates some directors because they think I am too open and can't play subtlety, but it is simply that every thought I have can be read on my face. Subtext is hard to play because my subtext, if I think about it for even a split second, becomes my obvious agenda. I have no doubt that my own mother could read my fear like a neon beer sign in a dark, sleazy bar, no matter how casually I reacted or reassured her that everything would be okay. She knew. She saw through every one of my defenses. I wish I had been stronger or had more faith or been a more capable liar. Not everything is passed down from our parents.

I tried to speak about the important things in that week before her surgery, but conversations were brief before she became exhausted and had to lie down. Mostly she was focusing (rather, obsessing—like daughter, like mother) on all the things that had gone wrong with her series of misdiagnoses. At first, the doctor thought her shortness of breath was from the missing lobe in her right lung—the results of a surgery for lung cancer a few years prior. Then the doctors insisted it was COPD, and then they said her breathing difficulties were due to her lungs filling up with fluid. She insisted it was an issue with her heart, but no one was listening, and my mother was never one to force her opinions on anyone who wasn't family. When I begged her to hound the doctors for quicker (or any) test results, she refused, saying, "No, they'll do it when they can. They're very busy." Her complete lack of trust in the medical professionals combined with her childlike faith and insistence on not disrupting their schedules was frustrating. I wanted to advocate for her, but she didn't want to ruffle feathers, even though she was certain the doctors were leading her down a fatal path.

Propriety. There is a way to do things. A right way and a wrong way. What looks good on the outside can often cover up the dirty secrets we have, the human flaws. Wear your jewelry and do your nails, and no one will see how much you are hurting on the inside. It's a cardinal sin to reveal a troubled heart for all to see.

I must have been a huge source of frustration to my mother, because my heart openly bleeds over everything I do.

CHAPTER EIGHT

JIM

Children often don't get along with their stepparents. Rip a kid away from everything she knows and put her into a new InstaFam without explanation, and the child is going to have trouble adjusting unless you talk things through, make her feel secure, and let her know that none of this upheaval is her fault. But parents in these situations so often want to forget the past and just move on. As I mentioned earlier, when my mother was done with something, she was done. There was no mollycoddling or explaining her feelings. It was just, "C'mon Cory, hop in the moving van. Here's your new dad."

But I didn't want a new dad. I liked the one I had just fine. The one who gave me the maraschino cherries from his Manhattans and hoisted me onto his 6'4" shoulders when we walked through the country club. The one who got angry when people asked (as they often did because he was fifty-six when I was born) if I was his granddaughter.

Further into my adulthood than seems normal, I had constant nightmares about Jim. I would wake up screaming or in a cold-sweat panic, crying uncontrollably. In these dreams I would be yelling at both Jim and my mother while they refused to hear me or see me or acknowledge my right to be angry. I'd wake sobbing, doubled over with rage and humiliation at being ignored. This repressed anger that was only allowed to burst out through my subconscious dreaming lasted right up until the year my mother died. Then the dreams stopped. Many days still, I'm so angry that my subconscious no longer needs to let it out at night. On those days, I rage enough all day, every day, and my subconscious, poor dear, needs some rest in the evenings.

It is strange to me to note that since my mother died, I've been the one who has ended up comforting Jim. I've been the one who looks in on him, helps him pack up my mother's clothes for Goodwill, and helps him decide whether or not to move into assisted living. I have never liked him, certainly never loved him, never asked him for advice or viewed him even remotely as a father figure, and yet here I am visiting to make sure he is not too lonely, secretly throwing away expired cans of food from the pantry to ensure he doesn't get sick. He seems to have revised our torturous history in his mind and now, after my mother has died, he calls me his "special daughter." I, who never sent a birthday card or acknowledged their wedding anniversary. I, who addressed their Christmas gifts to my mother alone. I, who called him My Mother's Husband but never my stepfather.

I don't know how to explain it, but a lifetime of revilement was somehow forcibly washed away when my mother died, lifted like a heavy veil. I still don't know how to reconcile myself to this broken man who slept only two hours a night and anguished over my mother lying in the hospital bed, talking to her as gently as one would a child.

The image of this haunts me. I don't know where this love and tenderness for my mother came from. I never saw it during the years when they were married, but now, suddenly, he seems lost without her.

Two days before my mother's surgery, I crouched on the floor of her bedroom while she sat on the edge of the bed. She'd been obsessing about the many disastrous medical mistakes and the long rabbit hole of misdiagnoses and wasted time that had precipitated her impending operation. She was starting to swirl about the surgery to come, and I could feel her panic.

"You know, Mama, there's a saying in the theatre: 'Bad dress rehearsal, great performance.' Maybe all these mistakes were your bad dress rehearsal."

Thankfully, that notion seemed to calm her just a little bit, though I didn't believe it myself. I knew in my heart that this bad dress rehearsal meant that the performance was going to be an unqualified disaster and closing notices would be posted on the callboard, but I kept my stage smile on for her, reassuring her that Death was not standing in the shadows of her bedroom, waiting for His moment. Oh, but I could feel Him, cold and hungry and impartial.

Jim walked into the bedroom and saw my mother struggling to wrap her sweater around her frail shoulders, and he reached over and gently lifted the garment and placed it around her. An act of tenderness. The first I'd seen in...ever. It surprised me, in a good way, but also in a "Why haven't you been like this to her before" way. It felt too little, too late. Where was this tenderness when he irrationally screamed at her for ordering cheese pizza for my vegetarian daughter instead of the sausage pizza he liked? So many years of hating him for never telling her that she was beautiful or that he loved her don't get to be erased just because he lifted a sweater to her shoulders. Do they?

Then again, maybe I just never saw the more tender moments between them. Or maybe I simply didn't want to see them. I am no longer sure whose history is the revisionist one.

CHAPTER NINE

MY MOTHER, THE CACTUS

T he day before my mother's surgery, I borrowed her car to drive to The Folk Shop.
Mama loved her red Chrysler 300: white leather seats, navigational system, a sort of opulent old-person car. Their other car, a Chrysler Sebring, was also red, by her choice. I used to tease her about having two virtually identical cars. Personally, I think if you are going to have two of something, they should be different so you have a specific use for each. Like, luxury car/economy car or backroad Jeep/ gas-conserving Prius. But Erni liked what she liked, and apparently she liked red Chrysler sedans.

They say that when you divorce a husband, your next partner will have all of the same problems as the first. Same issues, different penis. We keep reliving what we know until we finally learn to break the cycle. I wondered what exactly the common ground was between Mama's three husbands. Were they all cold and emotionally distant? Or did she keep her love at bay so that she couldn't be hurt? Was she constantly expecting them to choose something or someone over her, the way her father had chosen Nettie? Maybe these men were reserved, but I know they all loved her, fiercely. She was that type of woman.

When you are a child of divorce, as I am, you often learn to keep love at arm's length. You're always waiting for the fantasy to end, expecting your lover to leave you, because that's how love ends. Abandonment. That's the story you know. Moving halfway across the country to start a new life again and again and again. It's an unintentional consequence, but a lesson I learned well.

My mother moved to Arizona in 1989, the year before I got married and the year before my father, Tom Goodrich, died. By then, she'd been married to Jim for seventeen years, and she needed another new start. She finally got to escape Michigan, the state she hated. Mama was not a Midwestern girl. She was an East Coast baby, and the move to Michigan was hard on her. Not only did she have her two youngest children reluctantly in tow, but she lost the social structure she had grown up with: the country club set at Hercules; her sisters, Eileen and Joanne; and her bar buddy girlfriends, Marge and Dottie.

Michigan was (and still is) a sports paradise, with skiing and hiking and football, lots of football, lots of beer. She missed the culture of the East Coast—the music and theatre, the bridge clubs, the golfing, the pool, the daquiris, and the country club set with whom she had spent the previous thirty years. She deemed the Midwest socially backwards, and she didn't immediately fit in. Neither did Dale, and neither did I. Our new school friends made fun of our East Coast accents and our shyness. All the Goodriches have a wicked sense of humor, but it's dry and subtle. It felt like the kids of Michigan wanted something more overtly sophomoric. It took quite a while for each of us to find our niche.

Mama was movie-star glamorous, educated and articulate, and had a more, shall we say, enlightened view of love, sex, and marriage, though of course I didn't know those specifics until after she died. In Delaware, there were work parties that included booze and perhaps some sexual misadventures between the husbands and wives of the country club set. I've heard stories of blindfolded company wives being forced to identify their own husbands by feeling and comparing all of the men's penises. I'm not sure what prize the contest winner got, but it sure seems like all of the men were the ultimate winners of that little game. This was the Delaware my mother thrived in. But Michigan? Michigan was hardcore conservative. Midwestern pragmatic. A culture of steadiness and sensibility and side-eye judgement. In public, everyone watched out for their neighbors, and in private, everyone watched their neighbors.

After sixteen years of living in this puritanical midwestern society to which she never belonged, Ernie packed her bags and sold her colonial Ethan Allen furniture, and she and Jim moved to a retirement community in Green Valley, Arizona. Their new house was elegant and spare, and the view spectacular. The sun rose over the Santa Rita Mountains right in their backyard. I spent every morning of my mother's final two weeks on that back patio, coffee in hand, watching the dawn of each new day, fascinated by the ball of fire that slowly peeked over the crest of the mountains. Suddenly, I was flooded with light and heat, the quiet, blue cool of pre-dawn vanished with a whoosh, and everything was different. How often life is this way. Before and After.

I never understood my mother's love of the desert, so different from the lush green hills and meandering roads of northern Delaware. Arizona is stark and pointy and dangerous, though it is indeed beautiful. Everything that thrives there looks like it could hurt you: the cactus needles, the scorpions, the burning sun, the dry brown scrub on the desert. On that morning of the day before my mother's surgery, driving back from The Folk Shop, holding onto the joy I tucked in my pocket as I walked its aisles, I was flooded with appreciation for the desert's dangerous beauty.

On the highway between Tucson and Green Valley, there isn't much to speak of: a casino, a mine, the San Xavier mission. But there are thousands upon thousands of Saguaro cactus popping up out of the desert ground. They survive despite remarkable odds. These towering icons flourish in the harshest conditions. They protect themselves from thirsty animals with narrow, pointed needles, which hurt like hell if you run into them.

My mom was a cactus living in the shadows of the glorious mountains. She had built up spines to protect her, and she thrived in harsh conditions, without water or tenderness to help her grow. Maybe that's why she was so drawn to the desert.

She was fascinated by the Wild West. She voraciously read about the history and habits of the Native American Indians that inhabited this country before the white man came to claim it as his own. She knew where each indigenous tribe lived, what turquoise they wore and from which mine it came, and what types of baskets they wove and pottery they made. She sympathized with the cruel hardships they endured and the way of life that had been unjustly stolen from them. Her house was filled with Native American art, baskets, and jewelry. She wore only pastels and white, cowboy boots, and heavy silver squash blossom necklaces. She had finally found a new tribe where she belonged.

It was on my drive home from the folk instrument store that I felt a keen kinship with the desert, and my mother's love for this strange, nomadic land filled me for the first time. Finally, after twenty-seven years of her living there, Arizona got under my skin too. I felt a part of it. And I finally felt a part of her as well. How quickly that sense of security and belonging would be ripped away from me, and the sensation would be made worse by the fact that I had finally deeply felt the connection.

My mother and I had a complicated relationship. I suppose that is probably true of most mothers and daughters. You'd think that it should be the most natural bond in the world. I mean, you carry this little alien inside of your body for nine months; you are host to a parasitic being that lives off of your blood and nutrients and makes you crave ridiculous foods and throw up random others. You are one. Then you give birth, and suddenly, you're not. You are quickly two distinct creatures. But as long as that baby depends upon you for life, nourishment, love, and diaper changes, you are connected and complete together.

As the baby grows, however, something starts to shift. That cherished love thief starts to morph into its own distinct human being, different and complicated and oh so messy. You stop understanding them completely and start fighting because they mess up your house and your ambitions and your life. You love and protect them with a fierceness that would intimidate the most vicious lion, but you don't quite comprehend the things they do in the same the way you did back when they were totally dependent upon you. When they become their own person, you keep a piece of them with you always, but they are never wholly yours again. And, as the child, you sometimes long to crawl back into the meta-phorical womb, to have someone who knows and loves and understands you as she did when you were a part of her.

I feel guilty that I am angry at my mother. But I need to see her as the woman she was, making the choices she did, so that I can stop being angry. I don't want to have this much rage, and I'm pissed off that I do—which is the ultimate irony.

I want to yell at her. I did yell at her when I was a teenager. A lot. I wanted to understand the whys. Why did she rip me away from my home, my father, my life, only to be miserable herself? Had she been deliriously in love or showed a modicum of happiness being with Jim, I might have understood, but she was desperately unhappy with her new life in Michigan, and so was I. So was Dale. And rip-ping us away from our home for that mediocre half-life she endured was an act I could neither understand nor defend. So, I yelled at her. And she yelled back and told me I was selfish and there were things I didn't know.

"Then TELL me what I don't know. Tell me what made you divorce my father so that I can accept it and not be angry anymore! I won't judge you!" I'd yell.

"It's MY life, Cory!" she would holler back.

So, she wouldn't tell me. She never made herself a real person to me. She went to her death holding secrets that must have burned inside her with a fire hotter than the sun in the Arizona desert. And so it was up to me to unravel those secrets; to see her as the woman, not just the mother, not just the host. I was an alien in her world, and yet I needed to become a native of this sharply beautiful Mother Earth, so that I, too, could bloom in desert soil.

Jim and Ernie at Dale's wedding

CHAPTER TEN

THE STORY OF THE PANTS

1976—Clarkston, Michigan

I'm ten years old. We live in the house on Algonquin Road in Clarkston, Michigan, and I have become a chubby little kid. At school, Tom Hall and Eric Diebold make fun of me on the playground. They have a comedy routine that only ten-year-old boys can truly appreciate. They circle me and make fun of my belly and lack of sports acumen and ask me why I am so fat.

"You're the Goodrich Blimp!"

"You think you're so clever," I shoot back. "Goodrich doesn't have a blimp."

"They do NOW," and they run off, so proud that they've made me feel as big as a zeppelin and as small as a mouse all at the same time.

Eventually, I learn to mock myself along with them. I poke fun at my weight before they can. I laugh and call myself the blimp, and I triumph when Tom and Eric nod to each other and say, "You're alright, Goodrich. You're funny."

Victory. But at what cost?

It's around this time that my mother takes me shopping for new clothes. I hate shopping because nothing ever fits my body except for my mother's disappointment, and that I wear well. We are broke. Immediately after she and Jim married, they bought the house in Michigan, and immediately after that, Jim lost his job. He owes child support for his own four children, has a new wife, a new house and new furniture, two upset stepchildren, and a new job for half the pay and twice the effort. He is never around the house on Algonquin Road because he's either at work or attending classes for his master's degree. I don't mind him being absent. In fact, I prefer it when he is gone. But Mama is in shock from the Midwest culture and this new, lonesome, much less advantaged life. I hear her crying in the bedroom sometimes, in between the shuffling of cards for her endless practice games of bridge.

Shopping for new clothes for her fat, unhappy daughter, who was desperate for bell-bottoms and Garanimals in cute, snappy stripes must be a real treat for her. We find ourselves in a bargain basement closeout store in Waterford, full of last year's girls' clothes: tight jeans in eye-popping pink, horizontal striped shirts with no stretch. I walk into the dressing room with my mother and see her hide her disgust when not a single pair of jeans button across my soft tummy. "Hang on," she says, and comes back to the dressing room with an armful of blue jeans, none of them cute and all of them for boys. Not just any boys' jeans, but HUSKY boys' jeans.

Absolute mortification. Just kill me right here in the dressing room because there is nothing more embarrassing to me in this moment. Nothing, of course, except the word HUSKY emblazoned upon the jean tag, loudly proclaiming that I am not worthy. I am not a slim, I am not an average. I am a HUSKY. I complain, I pout, I do everything I can to not put those pants on my body, but my beautiful perfectly coiffed mother makes me because I need pants and we are broke and there are no other options.

I sulk, and when we get home, I throw the store bag on the kitchen counter and storm to my room. I'm ashamed, sad, fat, and a disappointment. How can I show up at the Camp Fire Girls picnic wearing these pants that will earn disdain from perfect, tiny Kim Kildal? The only thing worse than these nasty, thick denim pants is the shameful mocking I will get from wearing them.

I'm on the verge of panic, desperate to find a solution. I won't wear them as they are...but...maybe if I embroider a peace sign and some flowers on the back pocket...maybe I can make them cute and wearable?

I walk back into the kitchen to get the stupid pants, and to my horror, I see Jim parading around the living room, wearing my new Husky Boys jeans, modeling them for my mother. "Look, they're so big, they fit me!" he says as he saunters around the couch.

His body in my pants—the pants purchased for a ten-year-old girl but fitting a full-grown man. His body in my pants, mocking me in front of my mother who sits on the couch laughing, sharing a joke at my expense. They turn and see me staring, mouth agape, tears pouring down my face.

I run down the hallway and lock myself in my room. I won't talk to them for three days. When I won't come out for dinner, my mother begs. She says, "He was only making a joke," and "He didn't mean anything by it." She says I am being ridiculous.

I hate him, and by proxy, her too. She defends his humiliating behavior, and she let him pull the pants from the bag and not only watched as he put them on to make fun of me but watched and laughed. In doing so, she erased me.

Of all my childhood memories that fade into nostalgia with soft blurry edges, this one remains razor sharp. It still cuts, makes me bleed, and reminds me I am fat and abnormal, no matter what I look like now. I am something to mock. I am Nothing.

Now, forty years later, this is the memory that constantly comes to the front of my mind. I can forgive Jim for all the times he called me a Communist or made fun of my two left feet or criticized my acting on a TV show, telling me I smiled too much and the director should have told me what to do because I obviously didn't understand the text. For these things I can grit my teeth and (mostly) forgive. But putting on my new jeans and mocking me for being fat I was when I was ten years old, putting his body in something that was supposed to be, no matter how begrudgingly, mine, that I am unable to forgive. Or forget. And all these years later, the pain is so raw and visceral, I still weep at the memory. There are some wounds that are just too deep.

My mother wasn't the only one who would need her heart repaired.

CHAPTER ELEVEN

THE SHOPPING TRIP

October 2, 2017—Two days before the surgery

Mama wanted to go shopping to buy a robe for her planned stay in the rehabilitation center after her open-heart surgery. She wanted something light that she could easily slip on over the hospital gown and the bandages that would wrap around her torso. I knew she had something that would do in her closet already—my mother loved clothes almost as much as I do—but I realized this trip was about something other than necessity. She wanted to go shopping with me because, when everything was wrong, we could always bond over finding a bargain (unless that bargain culminated with the purchase of Husky boys jeans).

Mama dressed (all in white) and unplugged herself from the giant oxygen machine with its long tether tube. That cord stretched the entire length of the house, and I tripped on it repeatedly during my stay. I joked that we could never lose her; all we had to do was follow her leash to find where she was hiding. If only it were so easy to find her now.

She carried her portable oxygen pack out to the Chrysler 300 and waited in the passenger seat for me to chauffeur her around Green Valley. It was disorienting. I thought of all the times my mother had driven me (at about 15 mph) to Tubac or the White Elephant (a store much like the Goodwill) or her favorite Mexican restaurant in town. She never let me drive in Green Valley before, and she sat in the front seat like a child, waiting for me to take her to the store.

I knew she had very little strength, so we'd have to shop quickly. We chatted about trivial things on our way to her favorite bargain haunt, Bealls. I tried to steer her away from medical topics like the doctors' mishandling of her diagnosis, her need for a water pill for her swollen limbs, or what to do for her constant insomnia. There were a million things I wanted to know about her and her life, but the only question I could come up with during that role reversing car ride was one I had asked over and over again in my teenage years, one to which I'd never gotten a satisfactory answer.

What I really wanted to know was: "How could you divorce Daddy and force me to grow up with Jim? Did you know when you dragged me halfway across the country, away from my father and friends and home, that I would have abandonment issues and problems with commitment and men, and that I needed attention on the stage because I just wasn't getting it at home? Did you know that by introducing a new man into my life at a very sensitive age, a man who yelled and competed with me for your attention, that you unknowingly would give me lifelong nightmares in which I desperately screamed for help to no avail? Do you know that the reason I don't visit you often enough is because I don't want to deal with being called a Communist and fat, and that my husband actually consciously steps in as a buffer between me and Jim so that I can visit and talk to you instead of being the target of some misplaced hostility from your husband? Do you know how hard I have tried over the years to get past this, and how ashamed I am that I can't? That all I really need is an explanation and an 'I'm sorry'? Do you know how much I love you and how all I really need is for you to SEE me? To understand why this has cut and scarred me so deeply?"

It was a vast question and yet I didn't ask all or even any of it. Instead, I asked my mother with feigned dispassion, "Why did you and Daddy get divorced?"

I had asked this question so many times, and I always got non-answers: "Your father was a good man," or "He was so much older and I wanted to go out and have fun while he wanted to stay home," or "It's my life, Cory."

During one argument, I pushed and got just a tiny bit further. In her frustration, she blurted out, "There are things you don't know about your father, Cory." And then she locked everything down again. What don't I know Mama? What did he do to you?

But she remained silent.

I always knew there was so much more that she was concealing behind those vague answers, and whenever I pushed for more, she yelled at me to leave her alone. I was afraid to broach it all again, to dredge up all those fights we had when I was growing up, now that she was sick and fighting for her life.

But you see, in that moment, I knew what was coming. I could feel Death sitting in the back seat of the 300. Apparently, the son of a bitch had climbed in while I wasn't looking, and now, He breathed heavily on my neck, reminding me that He was waiting, so I had to very gently try one more time.

"Why did you and Daddy get divorced?" I asked, wondering if she would finally talk.

"I had an affair. You knew that, Cory."

Well, I wasn't expecting that bombshell.

"Well, yes, Mama," I stammered. "I guess I did know that, but I can't remember if you told me or if I knew... unofficially."

Here's what I knew...unofficially: I have a memory of being in a hotel room with my mother and a man when I was about three years old. In later years, I called him the Shadow Man because I did not remember who he was or what he looked like. What I clearly remembered was a door that adjoined our hotel room to another room. His room. I was fascinated that these two rooms could be connected privately from the inside instead of having to be accessed only from the long public hallway. For years I was obsessed with hotels that had these odd, secret, interstitial doors because I knew they were a clue to something. I just didn't know what that something was.

There were other details from that distant scene that I remembered: the carpet was a grayish green. I could feel its roughness between my toddler hands. I knew there was a crib set up in one of the rooms, and the Shadow Man stayed in the other room. This is how I "knew" she had an affair. Not because anyone had ever told me.

"Ok, so Mama, you had an affair..." I tried to say it casually, as if she'd told me she had a glass of lemonade with lunch.

"Oh yes. His wife came to the house once and asked

me not to take her husband. She was very nice about it. She was so well dressed, and she was very polite. I was very impressed with her."

Leave it to my mother to make a bigger deal out of what the woman was wearing than what she was saying.

"Wow. Ok, so...wow. And did you leave him alone?"

"Yes." There was no wistfulness in her tone. She said it simply, like a child who had been asked if she finished her milk.

And then I pulled into the parking lot at Bealls and the conversation was over. Just like that.

That's how it always was with my mother. She'd drop a bombshell of information like it was nothing, and then she'd be done and refuse to talk about it anymore. You'd be left reeling from this little breadcrumb she so casually tossed out, but you couldn't ask any more about it because, if you did, she'd get annoyed with you and tell you it was her life and her business. I learned not to push her for more but to take the crumb and squirrel it away, hoping that someday all the pieces would form a trail and lead me back home.

But here's the thing: You likely know where this is going. There would be no more breadcrumbs, because she died, holding the truth inside her. She never wanted me to see the whole picture or to find the trail. Or perhaps she thought I already had figured it out. Or maybe she left me the other pieces as a mystery to unravel after she was gone, to give me something to focus on to distract me from my grief. I don't know—I will never know what she really wanted.

You have to understand, my mother was sick. She was about to face the fight of her life, and I didn't want her upset. I didn't want her angry with me the way she was always angry at me for asking her questions about her life. Whenever I look back at this crystal-clear moment in the car, I wish I had Hermione Granger's time turner so that I could stay in the driver's seat, turn to look her in the eyes and say, "Mama, please tell me the story." But I didn't, because I needed to take care of her, to keep her calm. I needed to be the mother.

We walked into Bealls, my mind reeling with her revelation, but I tried to focus instead on finding her robe. She didn't like anything that was there, so we drove to a boutique that catered to the wardrobe needs of the fashionable lady retirees of Green Valley. Instead of searching through the racks herself, my mother went straight to the salesclerk for help.

"I'm having open heart surgery on Wednesday and I don't know how long I'll be in the hospital and after that I'll be going to a rehab center here in Green Valley so I need something that I can put on over the hospital gown—if I make it through the surgery."

My heart cracked open, hearing my mother babbling like a child, desperately seeking reassurance. She wanted a stranger to know her personal story, but she would never tell her own daughter her life stories unless the precisely correct questions were asked. And even then, she would dart and evade until we were both so dizzy that we forgot what the original question even was.

We never did find a robe. Instead, she bought a flouncy white cotton nightgown that buttoned all the way up the front and looked like something Maria Von Trapp would wear while bouncing with her future stepchildren on a bed during a thunderstorm. She paid full price for that nightgown that was not remotely what she needed. My mother never paid full price for anything.

That white nightgown is still sitting in the suitcase she packed for the rehabilitation center, washed but unworn. After she died, I found it, and I meant to take it home with me, but I couldn't. I repacked her suitcase and put it back in her closet. It's still there, waiting for her to claim it.

CHAPTER TWELVE

BAGGAGE

1971

I*'m five years old, and the fighting has escalated. Mama's full Manhattan cocktail goes flying at my father's head. He ducks and it crashes against the couch, ice and bourbon soaking into the scratchy blue upholstery.*

I go to the baby blue telephone in the kitchen and lift the receiver off the wall. My mother walks in and sees me.

"Cory, what are you doing?"

"How do you call the police? I need them to make you stop fighting."

"CORY! Put that phone down. Tom, she's trying to call the police. This is your fault!"

And the fighting starts up again.

They are arguing about me.

I go into my room, grab my blue teddy bear with the button eyes, my basket of stuffed kittens, and my pink satin blanket, and I stomp into the living room. "Can I borrow your suitcase, Mama?"

"Why on earth do you want my suitcase?"

"Because I'm running away, and I don't have one of my own."

"Do you see what you made her do, Tom?"

And they are back at it again.

I crawl underneath the dining room table and start singing the song I had written that year in kindergarten:

What color is love?
Is it red like a sunset, or blue like the sea?
What color is love?
It's the color of you and me.
If I could color the world
With crimson, orange, and gold,
I'd color a world full of happiness
And hands that reach out for one another to hold.

There weren't enough crayons in the box to color this household happy.

CHAPTER THIRTEEN

PHOTOGRAPHS

Winter, 2017-2018

I've had a recurring dream for years, a dream wherein I'm experiencing some sort of peril—a killer is chasing me, or I have to get home because I left my baby daughter alone in the crib while I've gone to a movie. In the dream, I am paralyzed. I can't move my feet. It's like slogging through ocean waves when the water is made of Play-Doh. It takes all my strength to move an inch forward. This is exactly what my depression feels like: a weight that wraps around me and makes it feel nearly impossible to move through space and time. All my life I have been dream-state afraid of what I am living through in the present. Walking the dog feels monumental. Putting on pants takes courage and perseverance. And everything is done with a side order of tears.

I'm not delicate. I am brave and bold. I am a woman of a certain age in a business that favors youth, after all, and one must have courage to survive that. I can perform in *front of a thousand people, even while in the grips of stage fright; I just keep moving through it. I take risks and put myself out there. I parent two girls and work and write and get shit done, but right now, in this winter after my mother has died, I feel like plankton, a one-celled organism trying to swim across the Play-Doh-filled Atlantic Ocean to another continent. It is all so fucking overwhelming.*

It's one thing to lose your mother—that's a milestone loss for nearly everyone. But to lose her in a traumatic fashion, and to deal with revealed family secrets and betrayal while going through perimenopause and financial difficulties and an identity crisis? Well, I'm pretty sure I have every right to feel like plankton.

I find myself going through my mother's box of memories and important papers repeatedly, obsessively looking for the piece of the puzzle I've missed. I pull out my Polaroids, family pictures, and childhood drawings, looking for anything that might give me solace or information, a clue as to why this all happened. I check the dates on her divorce papers and marriage certificates that I have never before seen, determined to put together a narrative of the woman who locked her past away. Depression and obsession—bound together as tightly as Thelma and Louise, they just might drive me over the edge of a cliff.

Mama was divorced from Tommy Hyatt in June of 1953, and she and Daddy were married on Friday, November 13, 1953. My brother Tommy was born in May of 1954. After doing the pregnancy math, you'll laugh at the obviously bad portent of the wedding date.

Susie was born eleven months later in April, 1955, and Dale came along in April 1959. A perfect family. I have so many pictures of the five of them on vacations or at impromptu home photo sessions. When I was a teenager, these pictures were kept in a yellow flowered cardboard box (the same one I found in Arizona, thirty-five years later) in the walk-in closet of Dale's bedroom in the house on Perry Lake Road in Clarkston, Michigan. Snapshots of them at the Grand Canyon or on an unmarked beach, or on the hearth of the fireplace at our home in Delaware, looking well-scrubbed and combed with pants and dresses perfectly ironed, my mother and father perfectly coiffed, as everyone always seemed to be in the fifties and early sixties. Occasionally, there is a shot of one child in tears while the other two smirked knowingly at the camera, but on the whole, they were happy together, those three perfectly timed children with their eternally glamorous mother and movie-star handsome father. The house was always immaculate, and so were their smiles.

Tom, Dale, Susie, and Tommy

Spring, 1984

    Mama and I are sitting on the floor of the closet, look-
ing at photographs. I'm a senior in high school, and Dale
is studying at the University of Michigan. Mama and I are
looking for a baby picture of me for a school project.

    The Cory photos are kept in a separate box from the oth-
ers, and they are not standard developed film, but Polaroids.

Cory, age three, with a real black eye.
You should see the other guy.

    I am dressed up in some odd outfit in almost all of
these pictures. It is obvious I am the clown, my mother's
dress-up doll. I'm mostly alone in these photos. There is an
occasional Christmas shot of the four Goodrich children

together, less than a handful of me with my mother, and a single shot of my father holding me as a baby. Other than that, it's all solo me—Cowgirl Cory with a toy guitar; or Guilty Cory sitting on the kitchen floor, caught with my finger in the peanut butter jar; or Plumber Cory in red rubber boots with a plunger, playing in the toilet. The pictures are funny and adorable and a little sad. Lonely. I envy the OGs (Original Goodriches) together in their trio pictures. I call these the "Back when the family was happy, before I came along and ruined it" photos.

My mother has no tolerance for my self-pitying commentary. She pulls out the box of Cory Polaroids and searches for the perfect shot of me as a baby. She's trying to find one that is unrecognizable for the "Name That Senior" baby photo contest we are having at school. The problem is, they are all clearly me. I'm President of the Drama Club and the lead in the school plays, so a picture of a costumed toddler is a dead giveaway, a foreshadowing of my illustrious high school years.

We find one that will suffice (which my classmates all immediately identified, incidentally) and then we go through the rest of the box for fun. I love when Mama and I sit in the closet and look at photos of the past because my life in Delaware has always been a bit of a blur to me. My memories of the early Delaware years are like these Polaroids, snapshots in time that were sometimes adorable but mostly a little sad.

I ask Mama to show me some of her own childhood pictures, and she says she doesn't have any. I've never seen photos of Nana, my grandfather whom I never met, or my mom's sisters, my Aunts Joanne and Eileen. I assume the

*pictures simply don't exist, not realizing that she's erasing
her past on purpose.*

*In the box of Cory Polaroids, I find two anomalies.
As I said, most of the pictures are of me solo, but there
are two photos of me as a nine-month-old being held by
a dark-haired man who is leaning against a car in a field.
His face is obscured and in profile, and I'm holding onto
his shoulder. He has a slight smile, but his head is down.
There is so much love in that photo. Also, a hint of sadness.*

This photo is labeled "Cory, 9 ½ months"

"Who is that man, Mama?"

*"Oh...just an old friend." Her voice gets soft and loses
the sharp edge I usually hear when she's speaking to me.
"Your father was jealous of him, so he had him transferred
down South. I could never forgive him for treating him so
cruelly."*

"Why was Daddy jealous of him?"

"Oh, who knows." She has recovered a bit of her composure, and the glass wall starts to roll up again, like a car window. "We took an art class together. Tom thought there was something going on, I suppose."

"Where is the man now? Do you ever talk to him?"

"He had a heart attack and died." Her voice is edged with bitterness, and it is clear the conversation is over.

I've already learned not to push. Not to ask for more because the door will inevitably slam shut, and I don't want to get my fingers caught when it does. But somehow, my subconscious records this memory: the way the light from the closet window catches a million dust particles dancing in its beam over our heads, the musty smell of old photographs and the way my mother turns inward, lost inside her memories. I can see her wheels churning, but she keeps it all inside, trying to calm the emotions that unsettle her, the emotions she can never share. My subconscious hits Record, so that thirty-some odd years later, I will be able to hit Play and relive that moment again and again, wondering why I waited for her to reveal her true self to me, why I didn't push until she cracked. I will constantly fear that if I push, she might break. And I will later come to realize that I was more afraid that I would be the one to shatter into a million unfixable pieces, drifting into the air like dust.

CHAPTER FOURTEEN

THE HOUSE
ON ALGONQUIN ROAD

When we moved to Michigan in 1974, our new split-level ranch was so different from the tiny stone house my Uncle George had designed and built in New Castle, right down the street from the golf course and Hercules Country Club. In Michigan, we lived in the woods on a dirt road that needed to be oiled twice a year to keep the dust settled. The house was relatively new—though we were not the first owners—and it had the most gruesome assortment of shag carpeting I have ever seen. I remember very little of that house, but I remember every inch of the dark paneled walls and psychedelic shag rugs. The wall-to-wall carpeting, both upstairs and down, consisted of three intermixed shades of blue, except in what was dubbed "Susie's room" (even though she never lived in that house) and my room. Susie's carpeting was a bright acid green and yellow, like a '70s floral print had vomited all over the floor after drinking too much Galliano.

But my room…

It was 1974 and we were approaching the Bicentennial of the United States of America, so Patriotism Chic was all the rage. My shag carpeting was red, white, and blue, and yes, it was as horrifying as you are likely imagining. Trying to make lemonade from lemons, my mother made me a bedspread out of a red, white, and blue patchwork calico. Very 1970s. Very Ugly. In every other square of the "quilt" was a cartoon caricature of Betsy Ross sewing the American flag. My mother made curtains from the same patriotic freakshow material. With this explosion of pattern thrown on top of that offensive shag carpet, you immediately have the prerequisites for American nightmares. No wonder I had constant insomnia and migraines. I hope whoever designed this catastrophic carpeting is in purgatory, with purgatory being a soundproof room with floor, walls, and ceiling covered by that disastrous carpeting.

Clarkston is a sleepy little village an hour's drive from the city of Detroit where Jim worked at the Chrysler plant. In the evenings he took classes to earn his MBA, so during the week I rarely saw him, but weekends were enforced "family" time—if one were required to call us a family. These weekend bonding sessions were always mandatory and often painful, as they usually consisted of manual labor of some variety. For months, bright and early on Saturday mornings, we drove to a forest littered with smooth grey rocks. My job was to find perfectly shaped stones and load them into the trunk of the car so that we could have free landscaping for our split-level shag-alicious nightmare. I was an eight-year-old, one-man chain gang. Find a rock, bend over and pick it up, wipe off the dirt, put it in my bucket, and when my bucket was full, lug it over to the car and dump the rock haul in the trunk. As the song goes, You load sixteen tons and what do you get? Another day older and deeper in debt....

On one of these forced child labor excursions, I had a question to ask about the rock I was carrying, I don't remember now what the question was exactly.

"Hey Jim..." I started, and he interrupted.

"You can call me Dad, you know."

I stood there, stunned into silence. I gripped the rock as though my hand were a vise, wanting to shatter it into sand. "Ok...D—"

I tried to say the word. "Hey, Da—," but I couldn't. The words stuck in my mouth like peanut butter. They wouldn't move. I felt like I had betrayed my real father by even saying, "Da—"

I never tried to call him Dad ever again. I always called him Jim. When my high school friends later referred to my "parents," I corrected them every time. My mother and My mother's husband. Never my father. Never my stepfather.

In those first years, my mother, her husband, and Dale and I often went on family vacations—meaning, I was trapped in the back seat of the car with my brother for days as we drove to someplace in which I had no interest and then drove back again. Thank God for books. I have travelled through most of the continental United States in the back seat of a Chrysler but have seen nothing but the inside of *The Secret Garden, The Chronicles of Narnia,* or *At the Back of the North Wind.* The inhabitants of the front seat would beg me to look up from my novel to see the mountains, and I would ignore them. Even if I wanted to see the cows or the landscape or the inside of Wall Drug, I kept my nose firmly in fantasy land, eager to escape them and the rest of reality.

One night in a Motel 6, while we were on another god-awful car trip to somewhere like hell, I lay in the double bed next to theirs, pretending to sleep. I overheard Jim complain to my mother that I resented him for taking us away from my father. I was only eight or nine at the time, and I lay there, eyes screwed shut, seething with anger. He was right. That was a part of it. I did resent him for taking me away from Delaware and Daddy, but I also resented him for who he was—cold, relentlessly demanding, a believer that humiliation was the best method of disciplining a child. I resented him because my mother was lonely, and I sometimes heard her stifling sobs in her bedroom during the day. I resented him because he put my stuffed kittens in a cage and put me in a red, white, and blue room that I hated. But mostly, I hated him because it was easier to hate him than to hate my mother. I knew who was responsible for all of this, but you learn to defend the people who hurt you the most because you simultaneously love them the most. Hating my mother was not an option. I loved her. And she was all that I had left.

My father, the epically handsome Tom Goodrich

CHAPTER FIFTEEN

MYTHOLOGY

November 2017—Chicago

Yesterday, I could barely move. The Play-Doh depression was so thick around me, every step was
painful and slogging. I hate being self-absorbed
or self-pitying, and that's what depression feels like to me:
a thick, weighted blanket of self-indulgence. I know there
is probably a chemical explanation for my serotonin levels
being too low, my bubble of coping mechanism protection
is depleted. I am just a raw, exposed nerve, but it bothers
me to be so needy and desperate. I hate that I want to be
wanted and need to be needed. This is my mother's legacy.
What legacy did I inherit from my father, I wonder?

Tom was always larger than life to me. A gentle giant
at 6'4", he always smelled of grass clippings and motor oil.
I rode with him on the tractor when he'd cut the lawn, and
if I was good and the mood struck him, he'd let me drive it
in circles around our front yard.

Daddy was a golf ball whisperer. He had seven hole-
in-one trophies kept behind the bar in the finished basement,

and his superpower was finding lost golf balls in the rough. His legs were incredibly muscular, and they were tan all the way to his mid-calf. Below the sock line his ankles were epically white. He was superhuman to me. Like Hercules.

Tom was fifty-six when I was born, and for the first seven years of my life he ironically worked at a company named Hercules, Inc. It was the 1960s, and the stereotypical breadwinner/housekeeper roles were carefully enacted, even when what was going on underneath was much less socially acceptable. Mama played bridge during the day, and Daddy played golf on the weekends. By the time our family unit had dissolved, my father had retired, and I spent the three months of summer break with him in the house on Hercules Road or at the Hercules Country Club, he on the golf course and I floating—white belly up—in the pool.

Hercules, Inc. was a chemical and munitions manufacturing company in Delaware, but in Roman mythology, Hercules (no Inc.) was a demigod born to a mortal woman and fathered by the god Zeus. A symbolic figure, his tales were an allegory to humans that even demigods must suffer humiliation and trials. Hercules always paid penance for his misdeeds willingly and gratefully, despite the fact that his superhuman strength and half-god status would have saved him from these punishments. He chose instead to act as a mortal with a human conscience. In the end, he was brought down by mortal fear and jealousy.

As the story goes, Hercules' wife, Deianira, was tricked by a centaur, the river guardian Nessus. After ferrying her across a treacherous river, the centaur attempted to rape Deianira, but an enraged Hercules witnessed the act of violence and shot the centaur with an arrow dipped in Hydra poison. As Nessus lay dying, he secretly handed Deianira a vial of his blood as an act of contrition. He whispered, "If you ever fear you are losing Hercules' love, use my blood as a love potion and he will return to you." The deceitful Nessus knew that the Hydra poison that tainted his blood would also act as a poison to Hercules, and this was the perfect way to take posthumous revenge on the demigod who killed him.

Eventually, Hercules took a young mistress, Iola, and a scorned Deianira feared that her husband was fonder of his new conquest than he was of her, so she dipped his shirt in the vial of the centaur's blood, hoping to regain her husband's love as Nessus had promised she would. The poison worked quickly, and Hercules, or at least the mortal half of Hercules, perished. Zeus took the remaining god half of Hercules up to the stars to live there for all eternity, immortal and valiant.

Hercules was poisoned by a woman who loved him, because he loved another.

My mother often said she thought my father had never gotten over his first wife, Eileen. I asked what had happened to her and why Tom and Eileen divorced, but got my usual non-answer. When my mother spoke of my father's undying love for his first wife, she sounded quite jealous.

Deianira soaked Hercules's shirt in the garnet blood of Nessus and, unintentionally, brought down a demigod. Ernie brought Tom down with a different type of garnet blood: Mine.

CHAPTER SIXTEEN

THE BOLO TIE

While I have never lived in the house in Green Valley, it feels so familiar to me. There is a unique way the house smells, and I recognize it instantly whenever I walk in the door.

I know every inch of the back patio with its epic view of the mountains because I've paced it a thousand times, either in worry for my mother or in angst, trying to get away from an argument.

I see my mother's decorating acumen in every inch of the white carpet and walls, the Native American baskets, artwork, and custom-made mesquite furniture. I know the paintings by Walter Stewart that were a carryover from our house in Delaware, and Daddy's silver bolo tie that hangs in a shadow box by the front door.

Daddy had a series of girlfriends after Ernie divorced him in 1974. There was Angela Alouise, the uber Italian who made her own homemade pasta and hung it to dry on the basement rafters. It was she who bought me the *Edith and Mr. Bear* book as I recovered from my tonsillectomy. Mrs. Alouise had jet black hair that she wore in a huge bun at the nape of her neck, and she was kind to me. She always loved my father, but that love was unrequited.

Then there was a string of women I don't remember. Daddy was a catch. Tall, blond and athletic, a champion golfer and former hammer thrower, he was naturally sought after by the ladies.

While I lived in Michigan with my mom, Jim, and Dale during the school year, the summer months were Daddy time. In early June, my mother would pack up our summer clothes and load us into whatever Chrysler car she was driving at the time, and we'd make the arduous thirteen-hour trek back to our father. She would take the long way to avoid driving through Detroit, and the first seven hours were filled with endless nothing. Ohio was flat and scenery-free. I of course lived in a book when Dale and I weren't fighting over the backseat—daring each other to cross the invisible middle line marking the edge of our own personal zones so we could punch whatever offending body part had entered enemy territory. Pennsylvania was more interesting because bur-rowing through the Appalachian Mountains were tunnels that looked like long, white-tiled bathrooms.

"Here we go!" My mother would always exclaim as we entered the tunnel. I was secretly afraid the mountain would crumble on top of us, leaving us trapped in the turnpike bathroom with its oddly flickering fluorescent lights.

By the time we got to Lancaster, Pennsylvania and the perennial stop for popcorn shrimp at Red Lobster, I started to get nervous. Would Daddy remember me? Should I hug him when I saw him? He wasn't the demonstrative type, but would that have changed since it had been nine months since I had last seen him? What would be different in the house? Was my room still the same?

We'd pull into the driveway around ten, and the fire-flies were the first to greet me. I'd escape the by-then tor-turous backseat of the car and try to catch one gently with my hands, stalling before I went into the house, stomach lurching because I did not know what it would be like see-ing Daddy again after such a long time. There was always an awkward conversation between Ernie and Tom in the dining room, and I would race around the house, taking a speedy tour to assess the state of affairs before my mother left us for the summer.

The blue living room and Daddy's yellow bedroom were generally the same, but my bedroom was always dif-ferent. The first year, it was stripped bare and there was only a double bed in the middle of the room and a card table pushed up against the mint green wall. My white Ethan Allen furniture had gone with us to Michigan, so Daddy bought a queen-sized bed to replace the two twins I had slept in when I shared this room with Susie. Everything else was gone. No more pink gingham curtains and matching pink bedspreads. No bookshelves that had housed my beloved stuffed animals and picture books. No evidence that I had ever lived in this room at all. It was now foreign to me, and I never slept well in that room again. It was no longer mine.

After the disappointment of my bedroom assessment, I'd peek out of the bathroom window to see what had changed outside. Before we moved, there was a glorious meadow behind our house filled with honeysuckle and brambles and ticks, and about a half a mile away Mr. Merz's old dilapidated barn leaned on a slightly treacherous angle. I was never allowed to go near the barn because it was in danger of collapsing. On the one occasion I disobeyed and explored the barn with my notorious rule-breaker friend, Ivy, I was caught. It was the only time my mother ever spanked me, with the pancake turner, no less. I've never seen her so angry. Eventually, that meadow was mowed down and sold to a housing development that planted McMansions where the honeysuckle once grew. There always seemed to be something new to mourn in the summer when I returned to Delaware and Daddy.

At the edge of the meadow, but still in our backyard, were three mimosa trees. I loved their smooth gray bark and the pink fluffy blossoms that bloomed like something out of a Dr. Seuss book. The three trees were named Tommy, Susie, and Dale. There was no Cory mimosa tree. Ivy and I would climb the Susie tree (that was our favorite) and pretend for hours that we were stranded in a jungle and this tree was our only protection from the cannibals and wild jungle animals eager to eat two tender pink children.

One spring, before I returned home for summer break, my father cut down all three of the mimosa trees. An abundance of pink furry flowers overwhelmed the storm gutters and gummed up the workings of his lawn mower. Discovering the trees were gone as I raced through my annual what-has-changed-in-Delaware tour was shocking. Little by little during my absence in the fall, winter, and spring, pieces of my past were drifting away like suddenly homeless pink blossoms. I was sure one day I would eventually return to find that even Daddy and the house had vanished.

One summer evening, instead of taking me to the movies or the Country Club to swim, Daddy brought me to meet Anita, the new woman he was dating. She was blond and trim and had Double Ds. Her apartment was glamorous: white lacquer and glass furniture, gold painted statues of Nefertiti on white pedestal columns, Lladró figurines, and intricate porcelain lamps with pastoral scenes of goatherds and maidens wrapped around each other in ecstasy. It was a far cry from the pious early colonial décor of the house on Hercules Road.

Anita tried to be welcoming, but she was clearly focused on nabbing my handsome father. The two of them lay on her bed watching TV and giggling like teenagers while I sat at the foot of the bed coloring and trying to disappear into the satin coverlet. Grown up flirting was mortifying. Anita knew I was the gateway to Tom, so she tried to charm me. I thought she actually liked me, but once the prize was won, I saw how much like the beginning of a fairy tale real life can be. The wicked stepmother always reveals her true colors.

By the time I returned for my third summer, Anita had moved in with all her shiny modern furniture. It never fit in with the rest of our house; Anita never fit into her bras or into our family. She loathed Tom's children—Tommy and Susie especially. She tolerated Dale because he was the level-headed one, funny, smart, and quiet. I worked hard to get her to like me, but I was never thin enough. To Anita, Fat was the Ultimate Sin, and further proof of my worthlessness and lack of discipline. She shamed me into dieting and her barely audible *tsk-tsk* was enough to make me swear off Daddy's infamous late-night chocolate chip milkshakes. When I excitedly told her of my dream of going into the theatre, thanks to her introducing me to the Broadway cast recording of *Evita*, she looked shocked and said, "But you're not *pretty* enough to be an actress!"

From that point on, whenever we would watch television together, she would pointedly simper, "Oh Tom, *that* woman is so beautiful. She's the type that should be on TV." She'd also point out the "ugly" women, mortified that someone ten pounds over emaciated was allowed to be on camera. She was a master of passive aggressive manipulation. Her constant criticism made me feel like a fat fish out of water in this house that was once mine but was now dominated by Anita's large persona and fake gold Egyptian statues.

Of course, we were probably subversive little shits to her. Tommy would bring his pet macaws over to the house and let them poop all over Anita's expensive Persian rugs. Upon Anita's declaration that she *loathed* Bach and preferred Chopin, and would Susie *please* not play Bach because it gave her a headache, Susie was sure to practice her loudest Bach piano pieces early in the morning, when their impact would cause the most distress. My friend Ivy stole money from Anita's purse when it was left lying around. I paraded around the house in my underwear, sashaying from side to side and cooing in a fake, high voice, *"Oh, Tooooom. Aren't you just the most wonderful maaaaan. Oooh, Tooooooooom."* I wanted Anita to like me, but I was secretly part of the Rebellion.

Years later, when Daddy died, Anita asked for his silver bolo tie, the one he wore with a white polo shirt every Thursday for roast beef night at the Country Club. She asked for the tie, ostensibly because she wanted something to remember him by, but mostly because she claimed to have paid for half of it on a vacation out west sometime in the late '70s. Anita had unexpectedly left my father a few years earlier and Tommy, as executor of the estate, refused her request and gifted it instead to my mother, which ruffled a few blond feathers. Maybe he should have let her keep it for the ten years she had stayed by my father's side, but I think it was his payback for all of the snide comments she had made to us over the years. The Rebellion finally won a battle.

My mother displayed that bolo tie in a shadow box by the front door of her house in Arizona, and while I was curious about the inappropriateness of her having a possession of Daddy's from the Anita years hanging prominently in her hallway, it was also strangely comforting to me to see it there.

It was the one thing I specifically asked for in my mother's pre-surgery "in case of" tour of the house. She made sure to tell Jim I was to take it immediately if she didn't survive. I have an immense sense of guilt for having it now. Maybe I shouldn't be the one to have such an iconic piece of Tom Goodrich. Maybe I don't deserve it.

CHAPTER SEVENTEEN

THE WRONG QUESTIONS

I am seven, and Dale and I are sitting on the floor in front of the giant TV console. I am about a foot away from the screen because my mother isn't home to yell at me for sitting too close. Mama comes in through the back door, looking exhausted and overwhelmed. I am unnerved by the weight of her sadness.

"Your Nana died this morning," she says simply, standing in the doorway, unsure of what to do next.

Dale and I are silent, also unsure of what to do. Then I remember the date.

"April Fools?" I ask my mother, hopefully.

"Cory, why would I joke about a thing like that?" she barks at me and walks into her bedroom and shuts the door. Dale and I slowly turn back to the TV. Neither of us say a word. Tears well up in my eyes, not only for Nana but also because I made Mama mad enough to yell at me. I hate when she yells at me. It makes me sick to my stomach to think I had failed her by asking if she was making an April Fool's joke out of her mother's death. I would have this same sick

feeling again decades later when the heart surgeon would
scold us about her undiagnosed A-fib. Like I had somehow
failed her.

My mother claimed to have strong negative reactions to many different drugs. If there were a weird side effect that only one person in a million suffered from while using a particular drug, my mother would be that one. Her own mother had this same oversensitivity to medication, and she was convinced this was what eventually killed Nana on April 1, 1974.

Because of this, my mother was impossible with doctors. She would never take a full dose of most medications, cutting the pills in half because of those ridiculous side effects she alone seemed to get. The doctors would scold her and write "non-compliant" in her charts. They dismissed her concerns, patted her on the head, and said, "Take it anyway, dear." And so, against her better judgement, she would take the medication and be rewarded with blood in her urine or a knee swollen to the size of a basketball. She would suffer for weeks before she could get a follow-up appointment to see the doctor, only to receive a prescription for a new medication that gave her a different but equally unbearable side effect. It was like the doctors blindly threw diagnoses and pills at her to see if anything stuck. I constantly hounded my mother, asking if she had called the doctor, but she demurred because she didn't want to bother them with her issues. I stopped pushing before she got angry at me, and would later curse myself for standing down. The Mother-Daughter Tango was punishing to us both.

In her last weeks, Mama was constantly anxious and short of breath, and sleep was especially elusive. She roamed the darkened hallway of the white house in the desert like a ghost, bound by the long plastic tube that gave her oxygen.

One night, in the days before her surgery, I woke from the uncomfortable white leather couch I'd been camping on in the den. That dreadful couch was barely long enough to allow five-foot four-inch me to stretch out. I had been tossing and turning, desperately trying to get back into a comfortable position. I stuck to the leather, the sheet fell off the back of the couch, I could turn over but couldn't scrunch my knees enough to sleep in my preferred fetal position, and I finally gave up. I stood to stretch my achy, bent legs and go to the bathroom. As I pushed the door open, I saw Mama in the night-light shadows, her nightgown hiked up around her waist, washing off the effects of the latest medication that gave her diarrhea. I backed out quickly, quietly, praying she didn't see me witness her distress; embarrassed (and bare-assed), vulnerable, and weak. She faced away from me, so I snuck out unobserved. The image still pops up in my memory, unbidden and unwelcome.

It was difficult to watch my mother become helpless, reversing our roles of caretaker and child. It is also difficult to wonder, *Why do I always seem to ask the wrong questions? Have I failed her again?*

CHAPTER EIGHTEEN

WORDS UNSPOKEN

October 4, 2017—The day of surgery

On the morning of the Beginning of the End, I went for a walk to help ease the stress of what was to come. I felt guilty for leaving the house and my mother even for thirty minutes. I came back and stood on the patio and watched the sun rising between the mountains, the cool early morning air blown gently away by the reaching beams of a faraway star, its oppressive heat invariably to come. The dramatic shift was a portent. Before and after. Everything hung on this day, this surgery, her life and death, my before and my becoming. I didn't know this consciously, of course, but I felt the reverberations of a seismic shift approaching, like the rats who fled the temples in Greece days before the quake destroyed the city of Helice.

We left for the Tucson Medical Center at 10am, and I felt guilty for insisting I drive separately from Mama and Jim, but I needed the space, the calm. The thought of being in the backseat of the car with the two of them reminded me of all those torturous family vacations, and I felt my body tense at the memory. I could not be a broken child on this day. I had to be strong for my mother. I had to be the adult.

I also knew who would climb in next to me in that backseat. I would not passively share it with Death, His encroaching robe surreptitiously crossing the invisible middle line, daring me to push Him back to His own side.

I also needed the freedom to leave the hospital only when I was ready and not at Jim's behest. I had the feeling that I would stay long into the night, longer than he would want to stay. I knew my duties should probably have included taking care of him too, and saving him from driving home alone, but I was defiant and resentful. I would take care of my mother. I was there for her. I would not split my focus to care for him. Amazing how we instantly revert back to our childhood selves when we are with the people who raised us.

The drive was long, and I was afraid. I gripped the steering wheel too hard and my left foot pushed against the floorboard until my foot cramped. I tried to breathe and remember to pretend to be strong. Fake it 'til you make it.

We got to the hospital, and I walked into the lobby with my mother while Jim parked their car. She was carrying her portable oxygen tank and she shuffled, but at least she was still walking on her own. Her fear was palpable, and she spoke like a child to the woman seated next to her in the waiting room.

"I'm having open heart surgery."

I recognized her need to tell people, to ask for prayers or help or compassion, and it devastated me.

We checked in at the surgical reception desk and they took my mother's list of current medications and asked me for her information: her address and birthdate. I had become her spokesperson. I was in charge, and I was never in charge. My mother was always in control, so it felt wrong to speak for her when she sat right beside me looking so small and scared. It felt invasive to dig through her purse to find her license, and to carry her belongings. She fretted about all of the past medical mistakes, and she harped on the fact that her feet and legs were swollen and her doctors should have prescribed a diuretic. Could she have a diuretic now? They spoke to her with patience and kindness, but her disorientation was noticeable. They treated her like a child, carefully, talking down to her, ignoring her concerns. She who is a Ruby Master bridge player, who gave birth to four children, who had three husbands and who knows how many lovers. She who traveled to all fifty states and twenty-six countries and knows chemistry and archaeology and Native American history is now patronized. How quickly we shift. Before and after.

They wheeled her away behind a door that said Do Not Enter to prep her for the surgery. They would call us when she was washed and weighed and gowned, the virgin prepared for the sacrificial rite. I pretended to be the grown up, but after she disappeared behind that door, I was the lost child.

When they called, Jim and I walked through the door marked Do Not Enter and were led to a tiny mustard yellow hospital room where Mama lied in a hospital bed, alone and small. We said little. We were scared, and any attempt at humor or lightening the mood fell flat. My mouth was dry and dull, and her skin was dry and cracking from the harsh antibiotic soap she was required to shower with the night before.

Prior to surgery, Erni was instructed to wash with a prescribed soap and sleep in a bed with fresh sheets to protect against post-surgery infection. She defiantly declared she would not use the soap because it irritated her sensitive skin, and she refused to change her linens, insisting she had only slept on half the bed and the other side was clean. I refused to let her refuse and told her I would change her sheets. If she got an infection after the surgery and I hadn't changed the bed or insisted she use the soap, I would blame myself, and she didn't want me to do that, did she? She stopped protesting. I changed the sheets, and she washed with the soap.

I found myself wondering if she actually poured the soap down the drain or if she wanted to sleep in used bedding because she was secretly hoping to get an infection, longing for everything to be over. She was housebound, unable to breathe. She had enough. "I lived a good life, Cory," she said simply. I didn't believe her.

The three of us were uncomfortably crammed together in the pre-surgery hospital room. My mother was obsessing over a broken nail. She was annoyed that she was required to remove her pink nail polish. Her bare nails were thin and brittle and peeled like sheets of mica. She rummaged through her purse for a file, and when she could not find one, she scratched and rubbed the nail on the bed sheet, trying desperately to file the jagged edge, to fix something that was broken.

The nurse entered and told us to say our goodbyes, and nobody did anything. Mama continued to ask for a file and explained again to the nurse that she needed a diuretic. The nurse's response was falsely cheery. "Ok, sweetie, we'll see. C'mon. Time to say your I love you's now." The nurse's job must be difficult—forcing families to part as they stall for a few more precious last seconds, knowing they may never see each other again in this lifetime. I hugged my mother and my throat closed. I couldn't speak. She held on awkwardly and didn't say I love you but instead said, "Thank you for all you did—for all the cooking." It wasn't an "I'm proud of you" nor an "I should have told you the truth about your father." It was a "Thank you for choosing me."

"Of course," I answered, my throat constricting.

I didn't say the words I should have said: "I love you, Mama." No, neither one of us said the words, but we understood it to be true. We were embarrassed to say the words because if we did, we would become emotional, and emotion would betray our fear. So we were both silent. The nurse rolled her away from me, and I called down the hall, "Go Team Erni!" The hospital staff laughed, and my mother waved as she slowly disappeared down the hallway. I knew my cheerleading was nothing more than false enthusiasm. I am a terrible liar and she's always known it, but she smiled wanly as they wheeled her out of sight.

I should have told her. Damn it, I should have. And she should have told me. So many words unspoken...

FUCK

October 5th—The day after surgery

They told me she wasn't in pain. They lied.

SURGERY

After my mother disappeared beyond the forbidden-zone doors, Jim wanted to eat lunch, so we searched for the cafeteria. It was relatively far away from the ICU ward. Jim has a bad knee and walks with an uneven limping gait, so we called for a shuttle, which turned out to be a golf cart driven by a retiree volunteer. He tried to entertain us during the ride by sharing the hospital's illustrious history as a former tuberculosis sanitorium. I wanted nothing more than for the man to stop his chipper chattering. I wasn't in the mood to make perky conversation. I rode on the back of the cart trying to ignore him, clutching my huge purse stuffed with the as-yet-unread book, *The House at Riverton* and my laptop, hoping not to fall off onto the linoleum floor as Mr. Super-Enthusiastic-Tour-Guide practically popped wheelies around the hospital corners.

Jim and I sat in a cafeteria booth, and a hugely pregnant woman shuffled by us, her IV and family in tow. Her partner rubbed her back and gave her encouragement. She leaned on the IV pole, exhausted, and smiled, waiting for her new life to begin as we were watching our old life end.

That IV tether didn't bother her, and she happily dragged it around the various people seated with their sad, gray, rubber hospital cafeteria lunches. She wheeled past the male doctor passive-aggressively berating his female intern for her incompetence, past the lonely old madman slumped over and staring into his bowl of soup, past the family of five chattering happily on and on about granddad's miraculous recovery. Through it all, Jim and I sat in uncomfortable silence and tried to swallow the sawdust meal because we were supposed to keep up our strength.

After lunch, Jim headed back up to the surgical waiting room and I headed to my second favorite place (after the folk music store): the coffee shop. I figured I was going to be in the medical center for many long hours, so I'd better get on a first name basis with the barista. By the end of the week, all the baristas knew me and inquired about my mother's condition.

Thank God for small miracles—the coffee was good. I may have had to eat rubber hospital veggie burgers throughout the week, but at least I would be satisfyingly caffeinated.

The waiting room waiting game was tedious. I couldn't sit still but I couldn't go anywhere either. I paced, but I was aware that my agitation was making the other families nervous. As I sat in the stiff family lounge chairs, I noticed Jim in my peripheral vision, sitting catty-corner from me. I was annoyed that I could even see him; I wanted to erase him from my vision and my past the way my mother deleted portions of her history. What the hell was wrong with me? How could I be so fucking unfeeling toward him, even in a moment such as this? I moved to the other side of the room to avoid seeing him, but even more to avoid my negative feelings about him.

I tried to stream the BBC "Pride and Prejudice" on my computer, but the hospital Wi-Fi sucked and Mr. Darcy kept freezing with particularly unflattering facial expressions while the stream buffered. It was low res and pixelated, but it matched how I felt so I pressed forward, getting lost in my fear and anxiety every time the movie stuttered and paused to load. The computer's spinning wheel of death was an ominous portent. I'd see that little rainbow wheel in my mind's eye constantly over the next week. Was my mother just buffering, or was the system going to crash?

Finally, after two more trips to the coffee shop, an aborted attempt at the second episode of "Pride and Prejudice" and a full two hours of the most depressing movie ever about Jackie Kennedy, the physician's assistant pushed through the double doors and called, "Erni Perkins' family?" She ushered us to a private room. She was blond, tan, and cheerful, and she looked like she was going to climb into a BMW with her sorority sisters to go on a drunken skiing trip in the mountains right after she was done with us. Strangely, her buoyancy calmed me. The surgery went well.

The doctor sat at the table, and he was optimistic. He had successfully repaired the two valves in my mother's heart. He was less happy about the results of the A-fib procedure and scolded us. "Her heart is so enlarged that it looks like she has been suffering for close to ten years. Why wasn't this found earlier?" Why indeed? Erni had been begging for relief for over two years, and not one of her many doctors had diagnosed her correctly, yet still, I felt the stinging blame of not pushing her harder to insist upon answers.

Despite our failure to get my mother's atrial fibrillation properly diagnosed, the heart surgeon was pleased with his work. He used the Maze procedure and made small incisions all over my mother's heart to create scar tissue. He sealed the leaky valves that were making her weak and exhausted. He fixed her heart.

More to the point, he fixed the hole in her heart. He did not, however, fix the whole of her heart.

Sometimes, I think doctors only see the things they are trained to see—their specialty—rather than the entire system, just as we see our parents as only parents, not as whole people. Erni's heart surgeon fixed the problem, but it wasn't enough to heal her.

The perky assistant ushered us out of the office, and directed us down the hall to ICU, to wait for Mama.

She was wheeled into the recovery room, pale, tubes coming from her wrists, her heart and, most invasively, her mouth. She was being kept alive by blood pressure drugs and fluids and an apparatus that literally breathed for her; she was so knocked out by the anesthesia that she could not do it on her own. The machine made a constant gasping wheeze as it pushed puffs of air into her lungs. The night nurse was handsome and kind and pushed drugs, adjusted levels, propped her head with pillows. We waited until fatigue overwhelmed Jim and he said, "We should go home now." Too early, just as I had predicted. I delayed. I hemmed and hawed and found things to do until he finally repeated, "Time to go." I started to walk out the door with him, but something held me back.

"No, I think I'll stay for a little bit," I said.

"There's nothing you can do."

"I know," I replied "but I'm going to stay a while longer. You go."

It wasn't a question, it was a declaration. I know he wanted me to go home with him, perhaps so he wouldn't feel guilt at leaving her alone in the hospital, but I was adamant. My instinct was telling me to stay.

After Jim left, I was overwhelmed and exhausted, awkwardly holding her hand in between the tubes and wires and the railings of the hospital bed. The nurse said she wouldn't wake from the morphine until around 4am, when they would try to take the breathing tube out, so I should go home to get some rest. Of course, I ignored the advice. I stayed. Something was nagging at me, and I couldn't leave.

My mother and I always had a connection. I wouldn't say we were close exactly, or had a particularly bonded relationship, but I knew when she was going to call me before I ever heard the phone ring. So many times, I would pick up the landline to call her, only to find her already on the other end of the extension, having just dialed my number. We just had an intuition about each other.

My instinct said that she would need me on this night, and I was right. I'm learning to trust my intuition more now. I have never trusted my gut before, because when people constantly lie to you about truths you subconsciously know, you begin to believe that your nagging suspicions and intuition must actually be paranoia.

On this night, I chose to listen to my inner voice, and sure enough, Mama surfaced like a porpoise from the morphine. She grasped at the breathing tube, pulling, trying to yank it from her mouth and lungs. She was anxious and hysterical, and the nurse and I tried to calm the wild fear in her panicked brown eyes, terror pouring out in tearful streams.

"It's alright, Mama. The surgery went really well. They fixed your heart! You have to have the tube in to help you breathe." She looked at me and I was glad I was there and that she was not alone. We locked eyes, and she silently begged me to save her.

It felt endless. This panic, the clawing at the tube, the fear. Her body arched and wrenched and her hands reached for the tube again and again. I tried to hold her hands and I kept repeating, "You're okay, Mama, you're okay," but I was crying and feeling her primal panic. The nurse finally gave her a shot of morphine and Ativan to calm her and she slipped back under, into the river of dreams.

I knew I had stayed for this moment, so that when she came to, she would not be alone. She would know that someone had chosen to stay by her side. I was the one who had chosen to stay.

Knowing she was morphined-up again and would be knocked out for quite some time, I thought it prudent to go home and get some sleep while I still could.

I drove back to Green Valley, delirious with fatigue and fear. The white dashes of the highway blurred and wobbled one minute, and I was sharp and agitated the next. I collapsed onto that dreadful short couch (Jim had declared I was not allowed to sleep in my mother's bed) and slept feverishly for four hours, in and out of the same river of consciousness that my mother was swimming in, only my pain was that of the metaphorical heart.

Early the next morning, as soon as I could down half a pot of coffee and shower off the thick hospital smell of disinfectant and nervous sweat, I was back in the car with my bag, book, and work computer. After an hour-long commute, a race through the confusing hallways, and a stop at the hospital coffeeshop, I was back in the tiny room with the tubes and alarms and machines. She lay still, with the endotracheal tube in her mouth and the ventilator breathing for her, lost under morphine's watery deep. She could not rouse herself from under the somnambulant effect of the anesthesia, and the ICU nurse had been unable to remove the breathing tube.

When my mother told her many doctors that she had an extraordinarily sensitive system, that medicines overwhelmed her, they sent her off with instructions to follow like a good little girl, but my mother had never been a good little girl. It was no surprise to me that she was (over)reacting to the anesthesia in this way. She was giving them hell for not listening to her, even now. We told the attending physician and the nurses (again) about her over-sensitivity to drugs, and this time, for the first time, they listened, absorbed our claims and parroted them back to us as if they were their own. "She can't process the anesthesia. She just needs a bit longer to work it out of her system."

No shit. We know.

It was an endless day. There would be no movement from her for hours, and then she'd wake in a panic, grabbing for the tube, desperately trying to pull it out with pleading brown eyes and arms reaching out to us, then falling back into unconsciousness, and this left us unnerved. Jim and I obsessively watched the machine, looking for the black lines that would indicate that the breath she took was her own and not the work of the ventilator, but those black lines were few and far between, not enough to sustain her.

Then would come another period of wakefulness and

silent pleading and grasping. In an effort to keep her from yanking the tube out, her hands were wrapped and tied to the bed like a prisoner. A captive. We were torturing her. She should have been off the breathing machine by now. She should have been awake and in a chair and walking around the ICU with the help of her nurses and her smiling family, but she was still under, fighting the drugs, in agony. They refused to give her additional morphine because they feared she would slip even further into the abyss, and now their primary goal was to get her off the ventilator before infection could set in.

"So, what are you giving her for pain?" I asked the doctor making her rounds.

"Oh, old people don't feel the pain of surgery."

What the actual fuck.

A hatchet had been buried in her chest, and she was split in two, poked, prodded, cut, and then sewn back together like an old rag doll. But she doesn't feel any pain? Are you fucking kidding me?

Liars. They couldn't help her pain for fear it would drag her deeper into the coma, so they lied, and I ran around like Shirley MacLaine in "Terms of Endearment" begging them for something to help her. I knew she wasn't coming out of the anesthesia because the pain was too great; she was going within because it hurt too much to come up for air. I knew because I knew when she was going to call me and when she had bad news, and I knew when she was hurting from the divorce, and I knew that she had been keeping a secret from me and wouldn't tell me of her hurts and her heartbreaks, and I knew that pain was there because I always knew what she felt.

And they wouldn't listen to me.
Just like they never listened to her.

CHAPTER TWENTY-ONE

DOWN THE RABBIT HOLE

Are we better off forgetting the details?
I started writing this memoir as a way to process my mother's death and remember the events surrounding it as they happened before coping mechanisms settled in to destroy the memories in order to protect me. But I haven't yet been able to write about the actual moment of her death. I've *been* avoiding it. I've *been* avoiding reliving those moments because writing them down will make them real again in my mind and bring me one step closer to a breakdown.

My mother went out of this world like she came in. "The Red Menace," as she was called by someone along the way—probably my father, made her own choice as to when to go. There was no peaceful exit, even though we were there, holding her hands and singing to her. A timebomb went off and simultaneously destroyed her body and my life. Perhaps that sounds dramatic, but I was simply not prepared for the devastation left in her wake or for the PTSD I experienced, like a soldier having returned from war.

I'll be honest: I was a little worried about my mental health in the months after she died. I was able to cope better when I was with my brothers and sister. Maybe something about being together again reminded me that, in spite of the years apart and the distance between us, we are still a family. We grew up together and got on each other's nerves as children (and still do now as adults). When we are together, I remember I am not just an interloper to their happy little trio. Nothing has changed.

But when home alone, or even at home with David and the girls, I still get a little paranoid. Obsessive. Worried that I don't belong to this family, and that there was a plot to keep the truth from me. To punish me.

I know this is not true, but my brain goes there.

I talk out loud to myself when I am alone making coffee.

I argue with myself. I start to doubt the information I've been given from various people, and I make up wild conspiracy theories in my head. I feel just a small crack emerge in my sanity, and I worry that another hit will blow that motherfucker wide open and I will fall down the chasm of insanity like Alice falling down the rabbit hole. Down, down, down, down...

1989, Lancaster, Pennsylvania

I'm twenty-one and I'm doing a national children's theatre tour of Alice in Wonderland. We are performing at the Fulton Opera House in Lancaster. For some reason, we have a couple of free days after this performance, before our little bus-and-truck production moves on to the next city. Lancaster is only an hour's drive from Wilmington, so I've

asked my father, Tom, to come pick me up so we can spend
a few days together before my cross-country tour resumes.
I arrange for a ticket to be held at the box office under his
name, and I tell him I will meet him out front after the show.

I am excited because Daddy has never seen me perform;
he saw none of my high school choir concerts or musicals
or college plays or cabarets. Nothing. I have only seen him
in his world—in Delaware. He has never seen me in mine. I
am thrilled that he will not only finally see me perform but
he will watch me play Alice, the title character in a really
charming musical for young audiences.

I'm nervous during the performance, knowing he is
there in the audience, but inside I am beaming. My father
is finally seeing me, the authentic me. Not the little girl
but a woman, a paid performer. I AM pretty enough to be
an actress.

I walk outside of the theatre after the performance, and
I see Daddy standing by the box office window. I wonder,
as I do every year when I see him again, if I should hug
him. I run to him and pause awkwardly, and he says hello.
I don't hug him even though I want to. I wait for him to say
something about my performance, and when he doesn't, I
self-consciously ask how he liked the show. "Oh, I didn't
see it. I waited out here."

It would be cliché to say, "time stopped" or "my heart sank
into my stomach," but those things happened. The moment
took my breath away—also cliché, but so true. All those
years I spent growing up five-hundred miles away from him
in Michigan, all the missed high school concerts, the leads

in school plays, the chorus solos—these were the things that defined me. And here was the one chance he had to see—in person—the person I was and the life I had chosen, and he didn't walk into the building. He was there, but he waited outside.

Sometimes, the things that most define our lives are not the things that happen, but the things that don't.

Daddy died a year later, so there was never another opportunity, and even if there had been, I doubt he would have walked into the building then either. It plagues me. Did he not understand how important performing was to me? Did he just not care? Was this the ultimate metaphor for my life? My father never saw me perform. My father never saw me. My father never knew me.

And I never knew my father.

"There are things you don't know about your father, Cory."

And this is why I worry that another blow to the tiny but delicate crack in my sanity will shatter me wide open.

CHAPTER TWENTY-TWO

PRETTY LIES

October 5, 2017—One day post surgery

I spend all day at the hospital with Jim. *Mama drifts in and out of consciousness, but she has been down deep most of the day. She wakes periodically and claws at the tube, but the breathing machine is still doing 95% of the work, pushing air in and out of her lungs. We are frustrated and heartsick, but the nurses and doctors keep repeating flatly that she is not processing the anesthesia in a normal fashion (duh), but it is nothing to worry about—everyone responds differently. I ask what they are giving her for her pain, and they say Tylenol and I lose my shit again. Tylenol doesn't even begin to alleviate one of my headaches, how could it possibly work on a body cleaved in two? They refuse to give her anything stronger despite my pleas, and I wonder if they think the sheer pain will rouse her from her coma.*

At around seven, Jim leaves the hospital to go pick up my sister Susie from the airport. He will take her back to the house in Green Valley, and I will sit vigil with my mother until I am too weary to take any more. I am curled up in the hard chair, playing music for her, trying to focus on my work as producer of a Christmas CD for the charity organization Season of Concern. Peace on Earth and Good Will to Men is about the furthest thing from my mind right now, so I get very little done. I crack open The House at Riverton *and read the first page for the third time, but I cannot focus, so back into my bag it goes. I hold my mother's hand and self-consciously talk to her. Can she hear me? What do I have to say, anyway? Will sappy declarations of love mean anything, or will she wonder who the hell this emotional basket-case child is? But I talk anyway and sing softly to her, feeling foolish but determined to let her know that I am there.*

Mark, the day nurse, is in and out of the tiny ICU room, and he smiles and gives me encouragement, but I can see he is frustrated looking at the numbers on my mother's chart. He has been adjusting levels of various medications throughout the course of the day, but nothing seems to satisfy him. I've asked him several times if my mother's condition is something he's seen before, and each time he shrugs and says, "I've seen it all." But now that Jim is out of the room, his answer changes. He wants me to know the truth because he knows I know he has been lying.

Mark is short and sturdy; a comfortable man. I've also learned he is a musician, so I instinctively trust him. He is the type of man you could lean on, so I do. "Mark, is this normal?" I ask again.

He sighs and sits down in the chair next to me. He takes my hand. "No. It's not. She is down so deep, and if she doesn't start breathing on her own soon, you are going to have to make some difficult choices."

"She doesn't want this," I tell him, shaking my head furiously. I can feel her not coming up for air, not breathing on her own because she wants to die, but you can't exactly pull the plug on an intuition.

"Are there any other options? Is there anything else we can do?"

"Dialysis," Mark tells me, "but we really don't want to put her through that. It's extreme." He takes my other hand and looks me straight in the eyes. "So, we are going to do everything we can to get her out of this before we go that route."

Okay...Dialysis—not a good sign.

I thank Mark for his forthrightness and his sympathy. He gives me courage by telling me the truth.

Here's the thing about the truth: It is usually easier to handle than a lie. When you tell a lie, the person you are telling it to usually knows, somewhere inside. They may not consciously realize it, but an uneasy feeling sets in. They start to doubt themselves and their instincts, and they know something is wrong, even if they can't quite put a finger on what that something is.

It works that way for me, anyway. I can deal with a hard truth. A pretty lie, on the other hand, is like walking in quicksand, every step pulling me further down and under, just like my mother is down and under in her postoperative coma.

Tell me the truth so I am not basing my life on a lie: Have you guessed my mother's secret yet?

CHAPTER TWENTY-THREE

THE ROLES WE PLAY

P erforming in a play requires a huge level of vulnerability. You have to crack yourself open for eight shows a week and pour out the pieces of your psyche that you often hide even from yourself. You become a channel for the emotional life of the character, a conduit between the playwright and the audience. You aren't yourself. The character's life is not your life, and her body is not your body, but she drapes over you like a cashmere shawl, inhabits your cells and looks and talks and moves just like you, and you move and talk and look just like her. You are two beings, but you are also one.

Sometimes it's hard, even for someone close to you, to distinguish between the character you are playing and the real you. But from inside, unless you are a method actor, you know that you are not the character, but are rather in service to art, to story, to communication. A method actor strives to fully *become* the role they are playing, living in their persona, remaining in character even when the camera is not rolling nor the stage lights turned on.

There is a famous story that illustrates the difference

between a method actor and a classically trained actor. As the legend goes, during the shooting of "Marathon Man," Sir Laurence Olivier (a classically trained stage actor) and Dustin Hoffman (a notorious method actor) had the following exchange during the shoot:

"How did your week go?" Olivier asked.

Hoffman told him that he had filmed a scene in which his character was supposed to have been up for three days straight.

"So, what did you do?" Olivier asked.

"Well, I stayed up for three days and three nights."

Laurence Olivier dryly remarked, "My dear boy, why don't you just try acting?"

That oft-quoted parable is a warning to actors who potentially take their jobs to dangerous, self-harm levels. Do we have to live our roles to do them justice? Can't we just try acting?

In my career, I have played the woman in a love triangle repeatedly. So often, in fact, that it is almost a joke: Guenevere *(Camelot)*, Laurey *(Oklahoma!)*, Mother *(Ragtime)*, Francesca *(The Bridges of Madison County)*. It became an unconscious mission for me to play these roles because of my firm belief that these fictional women were not immoral or loose. They had to make difficult choices, and the love they experienced could be neither controlled nor denied. I now realize I have been playing my mother, over and over again. I have been telling her story through my choice of roles, and I never even knew it.

The last show in which I performed before I went to Arizona for The Surgery was a musical version of *The Bridges of Madison County*, written by Jason Robert Brown and

Marsha Norman and based on the book by Robert James Waller. I played Francesca, the beautiful young war bride who married an American soldier in order to escape war-torn Italy. Twenty years later, a mysterious photographer from *National Geographic* appeared, and he and Francesca fell in love and spent three glorious, sex-soaked days together in rural Iowa. When reality set in and Francesca realized she had to choose between her soul mate photographer and the man who rescued her (and with whom she had created a family), she sacrificed intense, passionate love for the perhaps more noble love of husband and children.

I spoke with my mother over the phone three days before I left to rehearse for Peninsula Players in Door County. We discussed how important this role was to me and how excited I was to bring Francesca to life. I loved the passionate, swelling music and felt I deeply understood the predicament Francesca was in and knew exactly how I wanted to approach the role.

"Do you think Meryl Streep should have gone with Clint Eastwood?" My mother couldn't remember the characters' names, but she remembered the actors who played them in the movie.

"Well, the key," I told her, "is Francesca's devotion to her children. She couldn't bear the thought of ruining them, so even though Robert was her soul mate, she made the choice not just to stay with her husband but with the family. Her children are the crux of this story and her ultimate decision."

I don't remember how my mother replied, but I do remember the wistful longing in her voice when she spoke of how beautiful and heartbreaking the story was, and I wonder what she was really thinking.

"What did you think of Meryl Streep in 'Mamma Mia'?" my mother shifted topic. "I thought she was wonderful. You need to do that musical. That is really your show."

"Mamma Mia", the iconic Abba musical, is about a girl who has three possible fathers. She invites all three to her wedding, unbeknownst to her mother, Donna. I've wanted to play Donna for years, but I still haven't gotten the opportunity.

"You ARE that role." my mother says, and I agree. "Yes, Donna is a perfect role for me."

But now that she is gone, I realize she wasn't talking about Donna. She was talking about Sophie, the girl with three fathers. You ARE that role, she said.

I am Sophie, and my mother is Donna.

My dear girl, can't you just try acting?

CHAPTER TWENTY-FOUR

POUR MOOTH

October 6th—Two days post surgery

S usie arrived last night, and the two of us leave for the hospital around 7am. Jim headed out an hour earlier. He's been awake since two.

Susie is eleven years older than I am, she is an artist, and she's messy. A kind of leave-your-bags-all-over-the-house/ why-bother-with-suitcases-when-there-are-plastic-garbage-bags/focus-on-the-details-but-neglect-the-big-picture kind of messy. My mother, who is meticulous, who must have everything in order—no homework on the table, all things put away immediately—has a daughter who thrives in cha-os. She loves Susie, but she is bewildered by her. Susie is a free spirit.

Susie read the best bedtime stories to me when I was a child: The Chronicles of Narnia *and* The Hobbit. *She taught me to sing "Jeremiah was a Bullfrog" (with harmony) and to play piano. When my brother, Tommy, who was a real pain-in-the-ass growing up, interrupted my practicing, she made me a "Tommy-Proof Piano": a silent keyboard made out of construction paper so that I could practice in secret and avoid being teased and interrupted. When it came time to learn about the facts of life, it was Susie who taught me about Mr. Sperm and Mrs. Egg. She was different and cool, and I thought of her as my second, more accessible, hippy mother.*

On the car ride to the hospital, we talk about what to expect when she sees Mama: the tube coming from her mouth, the pallor, and the smallness of she who once loomed so large.

The conversation turns to lighter things. We talk about my daughter Celia and her special ability to connect with people who are in pain. Empathy. Her father and I are both empathic—we pick up the mood and the vibe of whomever we are with, and while it can be a blessing as an actor, it also kind of sucks as a real live person. I can be taken down by a stranger's bad mood in seconds.

Susie confesses that she has never understood empaths. "I guess I must be selfish. When someone tells me something painful, I generally only think about how it affects me. I am sympathetic to their problems, but the only emotion I feel is if it's going to change something in my life." This is curious to me. I think how freeing it must be to be able to divorce yourself from how everyone else is feeling. I ache at the thought of hurting someone, or someone being hurt. I know Susie is not callous; she is very sensitive indeed. But she does not absorb the same way I do. I envy that.

It's very tempting to rewrite history. And, like in a movie script, there were so many clues. If you saw them up on the big screen, you'd denounce the writers as being too obvious, too revealing. In acting, it's called "indicating." You can see the plot train barreling at full speed from fifty miles down the track. And yet, in my real life, that's exactly how it was: a thousand dropped clues, a hundred conversations that depicted character, all of them scattered along the way like breadcrumbs, but never examined closely enough to see that they were forming a clear trail.

Susie and I finally get to the hospital. I take her through the winding halls, past the coffee shop. Ok, I'm lying, I take her THROUGH the coffee shop because a latte can provide a tiny ounce of comfort when your mother is lost and no one can save her. Also, I am an addict. All things must eventually die, but my caffeine obsession will blaze on through eternity.

Eventually, we get to Mama's room. She is propped up in bed, and to our joy and surprise, the hateful tube is out of her mouth! This is the first positive sign in days. She is still coming in and out of consciousness, but she is breathing on her own. Susie and I put our bags down (not on the floor because never put anything on a hospital floor!) and I grab her hand and say, "Mama look who's here!" She turns to look at Susie and a voice I don't recognize slips out of her mouth and into the sterile air. "Pleeease. Pleeeeease. Please, Dear God," she rasps. "Pleeeease, Dear God," over and over.

"Mama, I'm here now. It's Susie. How are you?"

"Pleeeease, please, Dear God," she rasps, and Susie and I stand quiet. Susie has worked with the elderly in nursing homes, so she is not quite as rattled as I. The pleading continues for another ten minutes before Mama finally slips back into the quiet of sleep.

It's not unusual for someone who recently had a breathing tube removed to be scratchy and hoarse, but this high, thin voice is wrong in both cadence and tone. My mother's natural voice is warm and low and soothing. This voice, however, is Death and his crone, using my mother's body as their mouthpiece. I am shaken, unnerved, and downright terrified.

The next time she wakes, Jim is sitting to her right, holding her hand. "Pleeeease, Pleeease, Dear God. Jim, Jiiim, let me go. Let me gooooooo."

Again, it is the voice of the Death Crone, but this time, my mother knows full well what she is saying, and to whom. Let me go, Jim. Let me go.

We let those words absorb deep into our psyches, too stunned to move. I've had it. I stand up and grab her hand and force a fake cheeriness that I don't feel, would never feel. I am the actress, after all. "Mama, the surgery went really well. The breathing tube is out. Your heart is repaired, and you just need to rest more so we can get some food in you, and then get you walking."

"Pleease, please, Dear God." Over and over and over.

She is in and out of wakefulness all day long, and every time she surfaces, she starts croaking her leitmotif. Finally, Jim can take no more. He is upset by her constant pleading. He stands and says he wants to drive home before the sun sets. He has been up since two, unable to rest. Susie and I say we will remain in the hospital to hold vigil. After he leaves, Mama wakes and starts right up with her mantra. Please. Please, Dear God. Susie takes a position on one side of the hospital bed and I take the other. We start talking to her, trying anything to soothe her. Abruptly, she sits up and reaches both arms straight out in front of her to someone we could not see, begging, "Please, please, please."

"Do you see someone there, Mama? Is someone in the

room?" I'm frightened but also curious. Has someone come to guide her home? But she does not answer, falls back onto the bed, and starts bleating "Dear God, Dear God. Dear God."

Susie and I are at a loss. It's heartbreaking to watch her. Where is the manual for walking through the valley of the shadow of Death? Good Lord, tell me what to do.

"Mama, do you want us to pray?" *I ask.*

"Yes, pray Cory. Pray for Erni!"

So, we start. "Our Father, who art in heaven,"

"Our Father, who art in heaven..." *Mama speaks, firmly and clearly. The first coherent words we have heard her say.*

Hallowed be Thy name.

"Hallowed be Thy name." *Again, clear as a bell. Conscious. No delirium. Purposeful. Strong. I start to cry, but we continue.*

Thy kingdom come,

Thy will be done,

on Earth as it is in heaven.

And she repeats.

Give us this day our daily bread,

And forgive us our trespasses

As we forgive those who've trespassed against us.

Lead us not into temptation,

But deliver us from evil

For Thine is the Kingdom and the Power and the Glory,

Forever and ever,

Amen.

She repeats every line. And when we finish the prayer, she commands, "PRAY, Cory. Pray for Erni."

So, we do. Over and over again for an hour. We take

*breaks to sing "Mamma Mia" and "Tumbling Tumbleweeds"
and anything else we can think of to keep that wild panic
from her eyes, to keep her from begging us to let her go.
Our voices calm her agitation, but always, always she comes
back to "Pray, Pray for Erni."*

*Eventually, we are all three exhausted, and I know it is
time to go. I have an early plane to catch the next morning,
and she needs to sleep.*

*"Mama, I have to go home now. I'm flying back to Chi-
cago so I can help your granddaughter Celia get ready for
her Homecoming dance. She needs her Mommy, just like I
need my Mommy. Susie is going to be here with you until
I get back on the 17th, okay? I love you, but I have to go
home for a few days, okay?"*

"Okay. Pour Mooth."

"Huh?"

"Pour Mooth."

*"I have no idea what you mean, Mama. I'm going to go
now, I'll see you in a week, okay?"*

"Pour Mooth."

Those were the last words I ever heard my Mother say. Her
Rosebud. I still don't know what it means—maybe she
was asking for vermouth, but it only seems fitting that she
would leave me with yet another unfinished mystery I will
never solve.

Patterns. Plot clues dropped left and right, leading us
straight to the climax.

My mamma said

when she was dying
just before she's going on
Lord I'm just going over Jordan.
I'm just goin' over home.

CHAPTER TWENTY-FIVE

THREE ACTS OF KINDNESS

October 7, 2017

I *'m at the airport at 6am for a flight back home to Chicago. I'm on standby, so it's touch and go as to whether or not I will actually get back home. But my daughter has a Homecoming dance tonight, and I've promised her I will be home to help her get ready. I'm also scheduled to be in the recording studio on Monday morning for the annual holiday album I produce. The thought of having to capture Christmas joy while my mother fights for her life in a hospital bed feels surreal on this hot fall day in Arizona.*

I feel like crap for leaving my mother and going home, but I've been in the spiritual and literal desert for almost two weeks and I need time to regroup, take a breath, and regain my strength. I am encouraged by the removal of the breathing tube, but I am completely unnerved by the strange praying and the high, hoarse voice that was clearly not Erni's.

Once home in Chicago, I see my daughter off to her dance. She looks beautiful and the carefree exuberance of youth is like a clear, cold water stream. It washes away the desert sand, and I sleep for the first time in weeks—a long, twelve-hour stretch. It is sleep like death: deep, dreamless, and black. I didn't realize how exhausted I was. Susie texts me that Mama was up in her chair on Sunday and eating, finally. She is still not herself, but she is doing what she can to get better. She tries to eat even though she chokes on her applesauce. Her throat is still swollen from the tube, but she knows that eating is vital to recovery, and she is trying.

Her stomach was not the only place into which she got food. There is no way to be sure if it was due to the swelling from the prolonged amount of time with the breathing tube or exhaustion or lethargy from the anesthesia, but while eating, my mother aspirated applesauce into her lungs. She was still so weak and in pain from being sawed in half that she couldn't quite expel it all. She coughed it up as best she could despite the pain, looked at Susie sadly, and said, "This is so hard on you kids." The moment of clarity and compassion quickly cleared, however, and she was back to her cranky self, demanding to be put back into bed so she could rest. Her belligerence was actually encouraging to Susie. Mama still had her trademark feistiness.

On Monday, back home in Chicago, I spent all day in the studio, ushering talent in and out, having them sign waivers, doing producer-y things—which sounds impressive but mostly involves sitting on the couch in the booth, listening and eating snacks. I was scheduled to record a song for the album later in the afternoon even though I wasn't on the original roster. My voice was exhausted and wobbly, like an old church soprano, and I hadn't sung in weeks. But Eugene, my co-producer and pianist, encouraged me to sing for my mother, so I put on headphones and stood in front of the mic in the booth.

Ave Maria Gratia plena
Dominus tecum
Benedicta tu in mulieribus
Et benedictus, fructus ventris

Hail Mary full of grace
The Lord is with thee.
Blessed art thou among women
and blessed is the fruit of thy womb, Jesus.
Holy Mary, Mother of God,
Pray for us sinners now
and at the hour of our death.

I sang Ave Maria for my mother. A prayer to ask Mary to watch over her. It was not the best singing I've ever done, not by a long shot, but it was my prayer, and I desperately meant every word.

Ernie grew up Catholic, but she was kicked out of the church when she divorced Tommy Hyatt for being unambitious and lazy. The technical explanation may be that she was *not* excommunicated but was instead denied communion if she remarried, but the results were that my mother felt abandoned by her religion and her God. Small-town gossip and side-eye judgement never sat well with rebellious Ernie, so she left Catholicism altogether. I have never quite forgiven the church for that, for deserting her when she needed them most. I think of her strange and sudden request for prayers, for the Our Father. I choose to sing Ave Maria for her, thinking that perhaps even though the church left her behind, perhaps another Mother, Mother Mary, would not.

If you can save my mother, Blessed Mary, please do it. And if you can't, pray with me at the hour of her death. Please, Mary?

This is so fucking hard.

It is Monday night. I am restless, and I cannot sleep. I wake at 4am from a nightmare, and quickly realize I'm still in it. I get out of bed, make coffee, and decide to bake French bread because what else do you do at four in the morning when your mother is in the hospital and you can't be there with her? My intuition says something is not right, but I chalk it up to the lingering effects of the nightmare and reassure myself that my mother is on the upswing—after all, she sat up and ate yesterday. I go to my phone to reassure myself by rereading the text my sister had sent the day before, and then I see it: a voicemail from the hospital. My phone did not ring hours earlier because I had it on silent mode while I pseudo-slept.

They've called to tell me the breathing tube was put back in and that I should get to the hospital as soon as possible. I cannot comprehend this message. What happened? Shell-shocked, I dial the night nurse and push for more information.

Is it serious? How long do I have?

"You should get here soon."

My throat tightens, and I barely choke out the words: "But, is she going to die?"

"You should get here soon," the night nurse repeats.

They must get vagueness training in hospital school.

Some people are calm and cool in a crisis. They move swiftly and decisively, book plane tickets and car rentals, and pack while keeping a level head.

This is not me.

My hands are shaking so badly I can't even type the date into the Southwest ticket search engine. I am paralyzed as to whether I should fly to Phoenix or Tucson. From O'Hare or Midway? Do I pack a black dress, or is that too morbid? The analogy of running around like a chicken with its head cut off? Stick my head on that chicken's body and you have a pretty good picture of what it looks like in my kitchen. Flour from the half-baked bread everywhere, a dozen windows open on my computer desktop while I compare flight options.

Miraculously, I manage to book a flight and throw the unfolded laundry that I've just washed from the past week in Arizona into my suitcase (which is still half packed from the last trip). David takes me to the airport, and I book a car online while he drives. When I get to security, my bag is pulled for inspection. The TSA agent unzips the flap of my carry-on, and I see what my chicken self has done. Underwear and shoes; unfolded laundry; full-size bottles of my expensive shampoo, conditioner, and lotion haphazardly thrown together in the suitcase. She gingerly pulls out the large bottles of hair care products, looks at me in disgust, and says, "You can't take these in your carry-on. Where are you going?" Clearly, I am running from the law or hiding my illegal drugs and have to hightail it out of town in a hurry. I look at her and burst into full blown, ugly-cry sobs. "My mother is dying. I have to get to Arizona now. I have to get there before she dies!" The TSA agent takes one look at my swollen face, gently places the full-sized shampoo and conditioner bottles back in my bag, zips it up, and hands it to me. "Good luck." Her kindness makes me cry even harder, and I race through the airport to the gate, leaving sadness and used Kleenex in my wake. One small act of kindness...

On the plane, my despair and I are crammed into the middle seat. I'm agitated and shaking, and the man next to me starts talking. I am not in the mood, but my ingrained Midwestern female politeness won't allow me to put on my headphones to tune him out, so we start discussing the where and whys of our respective trips. He tells me of his ex-wife, the Playboy model who is now addicted to drugs and has alienated her children. When I tell him about my mother and her condition, he decides that he is going to take care of me. He chatters the whole rest of the flight to keep my mind from racing to the inevitable. He escorts me off the plane, to the shuttle, and then to the rental car facility so I don't even have to worry about where to go. He hugs me and wishes me luck, and I say, "Wait, I never even asked you your name." He smiles and says, "Tom," and walks away. Another small act of kindness.

I'm sure he is a real, flesh-and-blood man, but I am choosing to believe it was a divine message, my father coming down from heaven to take care of me. I don't believe in such things. Angels and serendipitously shaped clouds and dated pennies supposedly deposited from the beyond are too ethereal for my pragmatic mind. But this time, I don't care. I'm choosing to believe it was my daddy anyway.

I drive like the proverbial bat out of hell to get from the Phoenix airport to the medical center in Tucson, except I never actually get out of my own personal hell. I have beaten my wings to exhaustion, but here I still am, singed and tortured.

In the tiny, all-too-familiar ICU room, my mother lies on her bed, blue plastic tube taped to her mouth, even smaller and more wasted than she was three days ago. One eye is closed, and one eye remains open and staring. The eyeball is in danger of drying out, so Mark the Nurse gently places medical tape from her eyebrow to her cheek to hold the eye closed. I joke, "You look like a pirate, Mama." She does not respond.

Her hair, so white and soft, adorns her head on the pillow like Medusa's crown of snakes. The first thing I do when I walk into the room is brush it down to make her look more presentable to the world. As if it matters. But it does.

I brush my mother's hair with my daughter's pink plastic hairbrush, and I self-consciously tell her I love her, that she was a good mother and we were lucky to have her. As I whisper sentiment I was too embarrassed to share while she was healthy, one perfect tear drops from that taped eye down the side of her face onto the pillow. She isn't conscious, but I know she hears me and that she weeps, because that eye has been as dry as this desert she calls home. My mother cries as I tell her I love her, because she has been looking for love and forgiveness her whole life—from her mother, from the reserved men she married, perhaps especially from me. Maybe now she finally understands just how loved she truly is, how much I need her, how much I have always needed her. I hope my words give her peace and that she cries with me.

After my mother aspirated her applesauce, infection set into her lungs, and that infection is now coursing through

*her body. This is the official diagnosis, anyway. The un-
official diagnosis is that she was ready to move on. To die.
Please, Jim. Let me go...*

*But Jim can't let her go. There is one last-ditch effort
we could try, a Hail Mary play. We could put her on dialysis.
(Remember what Nurse Mark said, "Dialysis: bad.") We
could let a machine take the blood out of her body, clear it
of infection, and then put it back into her body. Cleansed.
As if any machine could purify her or absolve her of the
self-proclaimed hidden sins that she's kept locked in her
broken heart. Those "sins" poisoned her long before the
applesauce.*

*I know she wouldn't want this last effort to save her.
I know it. I can hear her pleading as loudly in my head as
I can hear the nurses' conversations at their station. But I
also know that everyone else needs to try. It isn't my decision anyway. As her husband, Jim has legal control over
her life at this moment, and as the most rational member
of the family, Dale's insistence we try this intervention is
reasonable. I, who have always been all emotion and feeling,
will turn down the volume of my intuition, knowing at this
point that it's more about them doing everything they can
to help her for our peace of mind than it is about actually
saving her. I have no doubt this is the right thing to do, but
I pace, I rage through the sterile hospital halls. I avoid eye
contact with the other patients' families because I don't want
them to see my despair. They worry enough over their own
recovering mothers and fathers and husbands. They need
hope, not evidence of what could so swiftly happen to their
family members too.*

The next three days are an endless nightmare blur. Drive to the hospital, sit by her side, drive to Green Valley, drive back to the hospital, sleep in the lobby on an even smaller couch than the one in my mother's den at home. At one point, while everyone else is getting lunch, I sit alone by her side, and Mark—the same nurse who earlier showed me a kindness by his gift of honesty—grabs my hand and pulls me out of the ICU room. "Come here. Don't ask, just come."

We walk down the hall to where a harpist has her instrument set up in the ward. Notes, beautiful and resonant and twinkly, wash over my body, cleansing me of a small bit of the hospital's trademark scent: antiseptic and anguish.

"Some of the patients don't like the harp music because they wake up and ask if they are in heaven," Mark chuckles.

We listen to the angel music, standing side by side.

"Thank you for this, Mark."

He looks me straight in the eye and half smiles. "You needed it." He squeezes my arm and walks away.

A third small act of kindness.

The dialysis lowers her temperature, and my mother is kept under a plastic warming blanket that looks like it is made of space-age packing bubbles. It feels like it's 150 degrees under there as we reach for her hand. She's in her own personal desert, but her body remains as cold as ice.

She will soon need that angel music to sing her home.

CHAPTER TWENTY-SIX

THE DAY MY MOTHER DIED

October 12, 2017—Green Valley, Arizona

As I get dressed in the early morning grey light, I agonize over what to wear to the hospital. Should I wear the bright yellow top to give people hope? To show that I, too, have confidence that she will make it through this ordeal? I pull it over my head and immediately strip it off. Hope is a lie.

I throw on my black Wonder Woman t-shirt and jeans, knowing in my heart that today is the day Erni will leave this earth. I hope it isn't too inappropriate to be so casually dressed, but I figure maybe my mother will recognize that I think she is a wonder woman. Maybe she will see that I would continue to be one too, and that she doesn't need to worry about me being strong enough to handle this. And then I laugh at my stupidity for thinking any of this really matters.

When we arrive at the hospital, they finally tell us that it's time to withdraw life support. In fact, they knew this two days ago when they suggested the Hail Mary dialysis play *that they knew had only a one percent chance of success. One percent. The cynical side of me thought they suggested it only in order to jack up the bill, but I know that is unkind. I know that decision was made for everyone's peace of mind, so that we could all say we made every effort possible. But all I could hear was, "Let me go, Let me go..." over and over and over again.*

After family phone calls (Let me go) and one last lunch in the cafeteria because we have no idea how long the actual dying will take (Let me go) and all the delaying that everyone can muster (Let me go), we quietly announce that we are ready. (I wasn't.) Mark and the palliative care nurse tell us to wait outside the room while they prepare my mother for her final journey. Jim walks out. Dale walks out. Susie walks out. I stay at the foot of her bed in defiance. I will not walk out. Not for one second while she is still alive. I will bear witness, Mama.

I don't blame them for walking out. They did what they were supposed to do. I am in the way, and the nurses want to spare my mother her dignity as they roll her helpless body back and forth, removing tubes and the catheter and stretching her out and preparing her for death. But I will not leave her. I cannot leave her. These are her last few minutes on earth. I have to soak up whatever is left of her.

The nurses finish their preparations, the breathing tube is removed, and we all man our positions. I stand on Mama's left and Susie stands on her right. Dale is at the foot of the bed and I'm not sure whether Jim is there or in the hallway. Her husband should probably be at her side, but I refuse to relinquish my spot. It could take hours, they say, but I know better.

The seconds start to lengthen between each breath. I know what I have to do, but I am scared because I know my voice will shake and it will be hard to get through. But what is bravery? Not the absence of fear, but having that fear and proceeding anyway. I start to sing. Softly, wobbly, my voice is weak with emotion, but I gather strength and courage with every note.

> There are loved ones in the glory
> Whose dear forms you often miss.
> When you close your earthly story
> Will you join them in their bliss?
> Will the circle be unbroken
> By and by Lord, by and by?
> There's a better home awaiting
> In the sky, Lord, in the sky.

Susie harmonizes on the chorus and we finish the song, but Mama is still breathing. There are endless gaps between each breath, but still, that faint intake rattle continues. Her mouth is gaping open, locked in position as if the tube were still there. It looks like a dark cave, and I can feel her soul hiding, waiting for the right moment to stealthily make its exit, unseen and unheard. I grasp for something to sing, but my mind is blank. All I can think of are fragments of Abba songs. Nonsense. Her favorite song is "Tumbling Tumble-weeds" but that doesn't seem sacred enough. I remember the Johnny Cash song that I sang in "Ring of Fire."

I believe my steps are growing wearier each day
Got another journey on my mind
Lures of this old world have ceased to make me want to stay
And my one regret is leaving you behind.

I'm singing my mother's soul to heaven. My final perfor-
mance for her.

And if it proves to be His will that I am first to cross
And somehow, I've a feeling it will be
When it comes your time to travel
Likewise, don't feel lost
For I will be the first one that you see.
And I'll be waiting on the far side banks of Jordan
I'll be sitting drawing pictures in the sand
And when I see you coming, I will rise up with a shout
And go running through the shallow waters...

Her heart stops beating.
Mark touches my shoulder and says, "She's gone," but
I will finish that song as her soul makes its final ascent to
God knows where.

...Reaching for your Hand.

Just like that, it is done.
And the rest of my story begins.

GRIEF

February 2018—3 ½ months post the Mom-apocalypse

I'm still grieving.
    Hard. Sharp. Fast and endless.
    You would think that the pain would, by now, be something more manageable. Dull and aching and not the sharp throb of an abscessed tooth, but every now and again I get the quick-intake-of-breath, drop-to-my-knees, shaking anxiety. I am processing, I tell myself. This too shall pass, and someday I will be able to look at this dispassionately and say, "Yes, that time was hard, but I survived." That which does not kill us makes us stronger.

But I don't believe it.

Mama muttered in the kitchen the week before her death, "My mother really ruined my life." And now I think, "Mama, were you talking about your mother? Or were you talking about my *mother ruining* my *life?"*

Those days in early October, the death of my mother and the revelation that followed have changed the landscape of my being. I'm afraid I will have sadness tattooed on my soul for the rest of my life. I will never be the woman I used to be. I am Before and After.

My mother's body couldn't process medication. My body cannot process grief.

PART II

THE LOST SISTER
DETECTIVE AGENCY

CHAPTER TWENTY-SEVEN

LEE

January 2018—Chicago, Illinois

I'm at the O'Hare airport, standing by the Starbucks next to baggage claim. Nervous. Heart lurching and stopping short like a teenager learning to drive a stick shift. I stand with my husband, but I wish I were waiting alone because I cannot explain the pull of what is coming through the terminal hallway, and I am reticent to share it. To share him. Some roads you have to travel alone. Spirit quests are always like this.

Is he the forty-something-year-old with the base-ball-cap-flattened hair struggling with his roller bag? The middle-aged businessman who looks tired and pissed that he has to wait to retrieve his luggage before heading off to the airport hotel for his double scotch and porn? Is he the short wiry man-boy with his backpack slung casually over his shoulder, headphones beating out the rhythm of his steps? It suddenly occurs to me I really don't know anything at all about the man I'm meeting, despite the fact we share

DNA. He could be a complete disappointment, but truly I am more worried that I will be the one to fulfill that role.

When he comes, I know him at once. I smile and point as if to say, "I recognize you!" but what I'm really saying is, "You are the piece I have been missing." He hesitates, and I glean that he is shy. Overwhelmed. Far cooler than I will ever be, wearing a punk black overcoat with a high collar that keeps the back of his shaved head warm and makes him look like a dark Victorian Lord. The rift of hair on top of his head is dyed black and cut in a severe wedge. Black pants tucked into high, lace-up boots, he is sharp, modern, European, like he stepped out of a nightclub in Berlin just as the sun is waking the earth, and suddenly, I am afraid. I suddenly know I am not edgy enough for him to love me. My suburban life, replete with two teenaged children and a household full of pets and homework and folk instruments are not nearly enough to hold the interest of this beautiful Goth man in black.

He strides towards me with his long lanky legs, slams his bag on the airport floor, sweeps me up in his arms and spins me around like a doll. My first words are classic Cory, full of self-criticism and insecurity. My first words to my forty-one-year-old brother, whom I am meeting for the first time: "Don't hurt your back."

The right words never seem to come. I am always so inside myself, so lost in my own worthlessness. I regret that those words were the first, but there will be many more to come. Countless I love you's said while staring at each other with wonder and gratitude for having found each other. Two lost souls united. He sees our father in my face, but I can't say I see the same.

I would love to say the knowing was instant; that the second we locked eyes and our bodies connected, that recognition would ease the awkwardness, but it didn't. We are tentative, each wondering if the other is judging. I walk ten feet ahead while he and my husband lag behind me, making idle small talk. How was the flight? The airport is busy. How strange this all is. I am nervous and I can't remember how to get back to the parking garage. I turn to look at this beautiful stranger and I giggle, and instantly feel foolish and immature. A big sister is supposed to lead the way, be calm and full of wisdom and guidance, but I have always been the little sister. I have always been taken care of and protected and shielded from truths that might hurt me, but now the truth stands before me and I am tongue-tied, nervous, and foolhardy for taking this spirit quest to him, to Lee, a brother I never knew and a stranger to me still. But somehow, we both have the deep instinct that we will be closer to each other than to all our other various and sundry brothers and sisters, because our father's blood rushes hotly through our veins. We are siblings, with a 99.4793% certainty. We share as many genomes as I do with my older siblings, Susie and Tommy and Dale. I can feel it. I know it. He is the dark angel and I, the white witch.

CHAPTER TWENTY-EIGHT

AFTERSHOCKS

October 12, 2017—Green Valley

W e came home from the hospital, shell-shocked. Susie and Jim stopped by the funeral home to schedule a consultation to discuss my mother's cremation, and I went to my second comfort zone, the grocery store, though I wasn't sure why. After all, I no longer had anyone to cook for. I wandered the aisle, thinking, "What is the point?" I bought a loaf of bread and a bottle of bourbon. We'd be drinking that night.

Since arriving the previous week, I'd been cooking up a proverbial storm. If you can't have meaningful conversations in order to avoid the obvious, then the next best way to show you care is to cook. It had become my mission to make sure my mother ate well that last week. She'd been complaining about Jim's cooking, which consisted of opening a can of (probably past its expiration date) soup. He had been complaining that he would ask her what she wanted to eat, and she would say, "Nothing," so he'd heat up a can of Campbell's for himself and nothing for her. Then she was hurt and probably sick to her stomach with resentment, so she didn't eat. She'd lost quite a bit of weight in the past few months, and I knew that hadn't helped her build strength for the surgery.

I also knew that, with my mother, you didn't ask, you simply *did*. I would say, "What do you want for dinner?" and she'd answer, "Nothing," just as she did with Jim. Despite her answer in the negative, I cooked (burned) something homemade like a butternut squash tart with spinach and pine nuts, or pizza on the grill, and she sat and ate a whole meal every time, despite her earlier protestations (and the scorch marks). You just had to do things for her, regardless of what she said she wanted. Service mattered to her.

And that's the puzzle piece that eluded everyone in the family. Dale often wondered why, when Mama came to Chicago, she always stayed at my house, never his. He'd complain that half the time she hadn't even called to tell him she was coming. I'd call and ask her if she'd told him and she'd say, "No, I want him to ask me to visit. I don't want to impose." It was a vicious cycle of denial and need.

I'm realizing now that Mama wanted to be *asked* to stay; *asked* to have dinner at her son's house. She stayed with me partly because I invited her and partly because she never wanted to be a burden to her son. Mostly, she wanted to be WANTED. She wanted to be chosen. And she would never force herself on someone who didn't choose her. I don't know what went wrong between her and Daddy, but I suspect he took her for granted and stopped letting her know how much he wanted and needed her.

It also occurs to me now that I am just like my mother. I didn't want to be a burden to her, so rather than ask her to tell me the truth, I wanted her to WANT to tell me the truth of her own accord.

This is so fucked up.

CHAPTER TWENTY-NINE

IS ANYONE THERE?

W hen my father Tom died in 1990, I expected to get messages from beyond. I don't mean ghostly visitations or pennies sliding across the table to say "I love you" Patrick Swayze style, but I was sure that my father would visit in dreams, that I would see him again even if only in my subconscious. If there IS a heaven or hell, I expect that parents are able to cross that mystic divide to say, "Hey, I'm still here. I'll see you again one day. Don't worry!"

In the twenty-eight years since my father died, he has visited me in but one single dream. The dream was something about a Viking boat (how appropriate...he was so mythic to me) carrying him to the other side. I won't go into more detail because there is nothing that annoys me more than having to listen to someone else's long-ass description of subconscious ramblings that make no sense to anyone but themselves. My point is simply that it always struck me as *odd,* this lack of dream state communication from Tom to me, his daughter. Whether his ghost wasn't talking or my subconscious wasn't listening, I'm still not sure.

What I also find odd are all the differences between my siblings and myself. Tommy, Susie, and Dale are all graced with Tom's height, and every one of them was blond as a baby, like our father, even though they have all aged into some shade of mouse brown now that they are adults. All three of them also have a reserved quality, something a little more cautious and quieter than my display-all-my-emotional-garbage-so-the world-can-see-it bullshit. I think they look at me with a bit of horror for exposing my soft underbelly so easily. I used to make jokes about the milkman being my real father, and they laughed right along with that joke because they all knew the milkman was not my father.

Every single one of them.

CHAPTER THIRTY

ERNESTINE'S BOX

Friday, October 13th, 2017—The day after Mama died

Mama has prepared for this. She sorted through the boxes of pictures and memorabilia of her life and shredded all of the love letters Jim wrote to her before they were married. Even though the marriage between Ernie and Tom had more or less disintegrated by the time these romantic letters were penned, they might still be a source of pain to their children, since the affair with Jim started while Ernie was still married to Tom. Jim kept all of her letters to him, but Erni (the one without an "e") would do whatever she could to preserve her carefully curated image.

What she hadn't destroyed and erased from her revisionist history was kept in the large flowered cardboard box in the bedroom closet. The three of us, Dale and Susie and I, were going through this box less than twenty-four hours after Mama had died. I insisted we do it immediately, even though I felt some reluctance from my siblings and Jim. No one was ready to go through her life's mementos, but I insisted I needed pictures to use for her Celebration of Life. In reality, there was a tiny seed of something nagging at me.

I remembered the pictures I saw when I was in high school of the man and the baby. I wondered if these photos were still in the box. Was this the man with whom she had an affair? The story of the well-dressed wife's visit, begging my mother not to take her husband, was like a small stone in my shoe.

The box was organized (of course it was) into sections. There are stacks of photos of my mother as a child with her parents, Antoinette and Caleb; another envelope with pictures of her sisters, Eileen and Joanne; a manila folder with mementos of her brief marriage to her first husband, Tommy Hyatt; and a whole album of their wedding pictures.

Tommy Hyatt and Ernestine

I had never seen any of these photographs—not when I asked to see pictures of my grandparents, or when I asked for details about her singing career. She had them the whole time and refused to show them to me. I was baffled by this secret stash of photos, and I am also blown away by the glamour and beauty of my young mother. The cheesecake bathing suit poses were made by a woman I never had any inkling existed. I have not inherited her glamour, but I have inherited her performing skills, skills that she denied ever having. The stacks of photos and reviews raving about the three singing sisters proved she was...well...not *lying,* exactly, but *omitting.*

Ernestine poses on the beach

Dale was sprawled on the floor of the living room, absorbed in reading a letter, and Susie and I looked through stacks of Tommy Hyatt memorabilia. Mama never told us much about him other than they were not married long and that the marriage was a huge mistake. When I found the divorce papers months after her death, the reason for their separation was listed as "unusual cruelty and violence." I am horrified at the thought of someone hurting beautiful, young Ernestine. That she never told any of us about it is confounding. Secrets. Erasure. If you don't talk about it, it didn't happen.

Cory, 9 ½ months

In another manila folder I found the two pictures I remembered from years ago—the photos of the mystery man and baby me. Tucked into this folder were also two letters from my father to Ernie, written about a month before his death in 1990. Not quite ready to focus on the pictures, I reached for these letters first, struck with the immediate recognition of my father's handwriting. It amazes me how something as simple as a person's handwriting can wallop you with the essence of who they were. It evokes such a visceral sense of remembrance.

I wondered why these were the only two letters from Tom in the box. Had she shredded the rest of his letters as well? And why were they kept in the folder with the photos of the strange man?

Though Tom and Ernie divorced in 1974, I had always considered it a congenial parting. Not that there wasn't hurt lodged deeply in both of their hearts, but I never, ever heard either of them disparage the other. Despite the pre-divorce arguments, the drinks flying across the room, the heated whispers, and the child placed as a barrier between them in the king-sized marriage bed, there was an unspoken love and respect between them. I appreciated that as a child. I was never made to choose one parent over the other in the divorce.

While I was in college, a fellow theatre student re-counted the horrors of her own parents' divorce. The judge had decreed that her mother was to get half of everything, so my friend's father grabbed the family cat and put him up on the cutting board. "You want half of everything?" he asked, and he took a butcher knife and chopped that cat in half right in front of his wife and daughter.

The cruelty of that moment, of seeing your father not only murder a beloved part of the family but also murder your image of him, to reveal this monster inside of him... it still sickens me. But this is what divorce and the pain of rejection can do to people: turn you into knife-wielding psychopaths.

But not *my* parents. No. *My* parents were civil. They still loved and respected one another, even though they had both moved on to other partners. It somehow made it easier to forget the fights and the memory of my mother locked out of the house by my father, as I pounded on the glass door and screamed for Daddy to let her in.

When Tom died on January 24, 1990, I was supposed to have been with him in Delaware. I had planned to visit from Chicago, where I had just moved several months earlier. David and I were living together at the time, and I selfishly wanted to spend time with my boyfriend. I wrote to my father, informing him of my change of plans. I mentioned that David and I were on the fast track to marriage, and he didn't need to worry about me. I hesitated before I signed my name to that letter. I wanted to tell him I loved him. I had never said it to him before, and I don't believe he had ever said it to me, either. That just wasn't my family's way. I wondered why we were so stingy with our words of love and affection. Tom once bragged that he had never said "I love you" to a woman. I don't know if this was said jokingly—it probably was, but it didn't surprise me.

I sat there in Chicago with my letter, stomach twisting, debating whether or not I should break family protocol. It seemed urgent to me for some reason, so out loud I said, "Screw it," and tentatively wrote, "I love you, Daddy" at the bottom of my page. It felt foreign to pen those words, as if I were writing with my left hand instead of my dominant right. My signature was small and apologetic. I sealed the envelope quickly and dropped it through the mail slot so that I wouldn't be able to take back my words.

A week later, he was gone. He had a heart attack, either from the blockages in his arteries, the stock market crashing, or the Philadelphia Eagles losing a game. I can imagine any one of these being the ultimate cause; he often became apoplectic over sports teams and finance. He lived alone (since Anita had unceremoniously dumped him and moved to Florida the year before). Consequently, his body remained undiscovered for two days.

Daddy died alone.

Daddy died alone when I was supposed to be there on a visit.

I was inconsolable. Had I been visiting at the moment of his heart attack, I could have called the paramedics, or maybe, just maybe, he wouldn't even have gotten so upset over a stupid football game. I should have been there. I should have been there when my father died.

But I wasn't.

Could have, should have, would have. Those "oulds" will kill you.

The first thing I did after two trains and an automobile brought me back to the house on Hercules Road was run down to the basement to Daddy's desk—the big blue desk laden with his bills and correspondences, the silver railroad tie commemorating his retirement, and the desk nameplate from his years at the chemical company. Had he received the letter I sent before he died? Did he read my "I love you"?

The letter was opened and filed in the "recently read" pile. He had.

My mother insisted she drive me to Delaware for my father's funeral. She knew I would not have been able to make that drive alone, and she needed the excuse to come to Delaware and pay her final respects to Daddy herself. There were some people who believed she didn't have a right to be at the funeral and the wake. That she had traded in her mourning wife card when she married Jim and packed us up in the U-Haul and moved to Michigan. But I knew without a doubt that she belonged there. I knew because she had been married to Tom for twenty years, and because they still loved and respected each other, because they had four children together, and because they still corresponded through letters that were filled with humor and pathos. Ernie belonged at Tom's funeral, and even if it wasn't the "proper" thing to do, it was the right thing for *her* to do. Most importantly, *I* needed my mother to be there.

I needed her just as I did after I had my tonsils removed and she was on her honeymoon with Jim. I needed her as I did every summer in Delaware when I was forced to be without her. I needed her as I did when I was terrified to go down into the basement because some invisible monster lurked down there waiting to grab me, and Susie was thankfully inspired to invent magic blue milk to calm my agitation and make me brave. I needed her as I did when I had night terrors of her dying and leaving me alone.

I needed my mother all those times, and she wasn't there. I sure as hell wasn't about to let her leave this time, no matter how disapproving certain members of the family might be. I needed her there, and she needed some closure. To say goodbye to the man who had swept her off her feet and rescued her from Tommy Hyatt, fathered her children, and never stopped loving her with all of his heart.

Ernestine never stopped loving Tom Goodrich, either. So, twenty-seven years later, when I found that my mother had saved two of Tom's letters, I wasn't surprised at all.

In the first letter I opened—one that Tom had written to Ernie several months before his death, the letter that my mother had carefully placed in the manila envelope with the two pictures of the mystery man—my father chronicled the travails of his failing heart and the numerous procedures he had endured in the hospital. He wrote of his fatigue and general malaise and of his recent ex, bleached blond Anita, who had ended their relationship by buying a condo in Florida without even bothering to tell Tom of her plans to leave him. He discovered this betrayal when the condo association called to confirm her moving date. Confused by the call, Tom confronted Anita, and she confessed her intention to end their relationship.

"It is definitely off between Anita and me. I was hoping to remain friends, but it looks like that is not possible either. I don't see how anyone could be better off without me than with me. Conceited? Of course," he wrote to my mother. He then thanked her for inviting him to her new house in Arizona and promised he would fly out with her sister Joanne to visit in the spring.

And then he wrote about me: *"I sent her an early $1,000 (theoretically her birthday present). I know how expensive Chicago, or any new place, can be and I won't let her have to worry about money. She is a wonderful girl and I am very proud of her. (After all, she is the only one who invited me to live with her when I became old and decrepit.) That promise was made when she was seven years old."*

Oh, I remember that promise. We were in Daddy's huge gray Thunderbird with the maroon leather interior. That car was a tank; it was like driving around in your living room. Daddy and I were on our way to Pathmark to get groceries. It was strange territory, my first summer back in Delaware after the divorce. I had never been to a grocery store with my father...and I doubt that, before the divorce, he had ever stepped foot in one himself. Now in this first post-divorce summer, he had to learn what type of food to feed a child. As a bachelor, he lived on Ritz crackers and spray cheese, sweet tea, rotisserie chicken, and nightly milkshakes. So I learned to as well.

It was on this grocery trip that Daddy first let me buy Lucky Charms—an absolutely forbidden cereal at my mother's house. In Michigan, the pantry held Raisin Bran and Fiber One and I wasn't allowed to eat the Raisin Bran because it was "Jim's cereal." In Delaware it was sugary cereal, mini bottles of Coke, and giant Hershey bars that were kept in the basement freezer. I may have been emotionally bereft, missing my mother, but I was well sugared up for those hot summer months.

As we drove to Pathmark, my Daddy called me his Little Buddy. I was like Gilligan with the Skipper, and I felt about as clumsy and ignorant. Daddy asked me what I wanted to be when I grew up and I don't remember my answer—it was probably something about being on TV—and he said, "You know you could be a lawyer if you wanted. You're smart enough, you could be anything you wanted to be."

Daddy had wanted to go to law school. He had, in fact, gotten a full ride to Harvard, but he lacked the money for books and the train fare to get to Cambridge. It was his biggest regret. Tom was a man of *almosts*. He *almost* went to law school. He *almost* qualified for the Olympics, he was *almost* a Rhodes Scholar. But the rules were changed the year he became eligible, and he did not meet the new requirements.

"Yeah, maybe I will be a lawyer. And you can come live with me."

"You won't want me to live with you. You'll live with your husband."

"Nope, you can come live with me when you are old and decrepit. My husband won't mind."

He was tickled, and probably amused that I knew the word decrepit.

This memory flooded back as I read the letter, sitting on the floor of the house in Green Valley. I knew Mama had kept this letter for me, specifically so that I would know how much my father had loved me. I started crying, not only from Daddy's words but from this prescient thoughtfulness of hers, to save this letter for me to find after she was gone.

The other letter from Tom was of a similar vein. I returned it to its envelope and turned my attention to the two photos also filed in the folder. I stared at the image of the strange man holding me. This is what I had been hoping to find, though I wasn't sure why.

Ten years earlier, my mother had brought me a box of my old drawings and school assignments when she came for one of her Chicago visits. I sat on the floor of my kitchen, going through the box as she watched, laughing at my early poems about love. She also included a portion of my baby Polaroids, and I secretly hoped she had included the photo of the shadow man, even then. I was disappointed that she hadn't, but I never asked her about it. Why was this photo—a photo I had seen only once—so deeply lodged in my memory?

And now, finally, the day after my mother's death, I found it again.

"HEY! You guys...did I tell you what Mama said to me last week?"

I recounted the strange car conversation; Mama admitting to having an affair and to the wife's visit to the house, begging Ernie to leave her husband alone. Being eleven and seven years older than I, respectively, I knew Susie and Dale might have some of the goods, some of the details about this man and his wife's visitation. I asked them repeatedly over the years why our parents had divorced, but they were always vague and claimed they remembered little of that time. They were so like our mother.

"You both were old enough to remember... Do you know about the affair? Is this the guy?"

Dale didn't move a muscle, but I felt a strange, cold tension.

"Yes, that's him."

They DO remember!

"Well, who is he!?"

I was secretly impressed that despite recently having a baby (me), my mom was still able to catch the eye and heart of the mystery man. Go Team Ernie, indeed.

"His name is Don Garnett," Dale answered quietly.

It slipped out quickly. No pause to reach for the name from the cobwebbed corners of his mind. No "I was too young to remember." This has caused him pain. I felt it.

"Really!? You know his name. What else do you remember about him?" I asked.

"How much do you want to know?"

Well that was an odd question.

"Everything..." I replied, but the ground tilted a bit because suddenly I knew.

"You used to call him Daddy Don."

And the floor dropped out from under me, like I'd been standing on a swinging trap door and they'd released the safety.

I know. I know. I know.

"Is he my real father?" The question floated out of me, as though I had always known, but of course I hadn't. Had I?

"Yes. I think so."

And the Earth spun off its axis into the dark, black void of the universe.

CHAPTER THIRTY-ONE

SOMEWHERE ON THE SIDE OF THE ROAD

Somewhere in the back of my mind, I knew.

I knew it when I joked about being the milkman's child. I knew it when I sat on the couch in Delaware, looking at the moon through the picture window, wondering where the man who could fill my emptiness might be.

I knew it when I wrote a song about Daddy (Tom) being a "diamond in the rough" and sang it for my mother in my music studio, daring her to contradict me and refute my claims of Daddy's perfection.

I knew it when she said, "There are things you don't know about your father, Cory."

I knew it when I saw those very same pictures when I was in high school.

I knew it in the week before her death when I wrote poems in my journal asking if I "would always be a question mark."

I knew when I had the memory of the hotel's green carpet and the adjoining door that connected me and my mother to the Shadow Man.

I knew it when I recalled my mother's favorite story

about my falling into a large fountain and a stranger just happening to swoop in and rescue me from drowning, always knowing somehow that the hero wasn't a stranger. He was familiar.

I knew it after my daughter Celia was born, blond and blue eyed, and I said, "She looks like Daddy, don't you think?" and my mother snorted and firmly stated, "NO."

I knew. But I didn't. I never put it together fully in my mind until that moment when everything suddenly came into sharp, telescoping focus.

The world was spinning, and I had no idea how to right it.

Dale walked over to his backpack and pulled out a third letter, the one he was reading while I read my Daddy's last letters to Ernie.

"This was in the folder with those pictures. When I realized who it was from, I hid it in my bag. I couldn't look at all of it. It was too painful to read. Look at the last page."

The letter was addressed to Ernie Perkins, and the postmark was dated 1976. It was signed, "Love, Don." I won't share the contents of that letter with you here. It is too personal, and it feels too invasive of both Don's and Ernie's privacy. Now this letter is mine to cherish and protect—the only keepsake of a father I can never have.

This letter is precious to me because it confirms that Don Garnett desperately loved my mother. It was written nine years after my birth, and two years after Ernie married Jim and I was dragged unwillingly to a new life in Michigan. Don missed his "most loved child." He wrote that, in his melancholic state, the only thing capable of giving him joy was looking forward to grandchildren descended from the two of them; descended from him and the woman he loved.

From him and Ernie. He closed the letter with "I hope you and Cory are well. Love, Don."

I hope you and *Cory* are well.

I was Donald Garnett's daughter. I was that most loved child. And I had the two grandchildren that this man so dearly looked forward to. Grandchildren he never knew. It was overwhelming; I couldn't catch my breath.

My mother, who had carefully curated the box of memories that would be the summation of her life, kept two pictures of me with my biological father, and a letter in his own handwriting that proved who he was and that he knew and loved me, his daughter. My mother wanted me to know who the Shadow Man was, and she wanted me to know who I was. Whose daughter I was. But she couldn't, or wouldn't, tell me herself. She left me to discover the truth without her. Alone.

Again.

I could not stay a second longer in the white house with the kachina dolls in the transom windows. I stood up from the floor that barely supported me, and sputtered something about needing to get some air and go for a drive. As I moved toward the garage, Dale stopped me. "Look, we don't know if this is true. You could still be Daddy's child. They were still together when you were born. I'm not even sure how I remember Don Garnett's name or if it is even correct."

I shook my head. "Then why was it so burned into your brain that it came out so easily after fifty-one years?"

Dale looked pained.

"I remember his name because I overheard it mentioned in so many of Mama and Daddy's arguments before they were divorced. I remember Daddy locking Mama out of the house and threatening to tell everyone *the truth about Cory."*

The Truth About Me. I was about to throw up on the white carpet. Mama would have killed me for messing up her decor, so I tried to escape to the car and safety, away from family secrets and the house that still smelled like my mother's perfume. I grabbed my purse from the counter. Maybe it wasn't true.

But then Susie reluctantly stood up and said, "Wait, I have to tell you something." Oh no. No, please, no Susie.

"I've known since you were two. Mama told me when I was thirteen that she and Daddy were fighting because Daddy was not your father. Your real father is Don Garnett."

Confirmation.

And betrayal...so sharp, like a slap across the face right after you've come in from the snow. It stung. Left an invisible red mark on my heart.

"She told you when you were thirteen? Why would she do that? That must have been a horrible burden for you to bear, keeping her secret."

"Well, no. She never asked me to keep it a secret."

Wait, what?

"Then why did you not tell me this before now? Don't you remember all those times I asked you about their divorce or told you about my memory of the hotel room with the adjoining doors and how I suspected she may have had an affair?" I had been pumping Susie for information for as long as I could remember, looking for something—though I didn't know what—and she turned out to be as taciturn and revisionist as my mother.

Her next statement wasn't flippant or thoughtless, though it may seem that way in print. She was pained, trying to sort through the details, questioning her own motivations.

"I didn't know why. I guess I just thought it was a special thing Mama and I shared between us. How could I reveal her secret when she trusted me with it?"

Susie was thirteen years old. A child. She needed that elusive bond with our mother too. She needed to protect her. I understood.

But it was still treason.

"I have to go. I can't be here right now..."

I grabbed the keys before I broke down in front of them, got in my mother's Sebring, and started to drive.

I had no idea where to go. I knew how to get to three places in Arizona: the grocery store, the hospital, and The Folk Shop. The Folk Shop where there were ukuleles and chords and structure and old-time music that dealt with heartbreak and despair and hunger and war. It was the only place I knew to go to soothe my broken soul.

You gotta walk that lonesome valley
You gotta walk it by yourself
Nobody else can walk it for you
You gotta walk that lonesome valley by yourself...

I drove blindly, that tune playing in my head on a relentless, unending loop. I was swirling, not sure what was down-side up or right-side down.

Not only was Tom not my biological father, but they *knew*, or at the very least, *suspected*. They all knew, and no one wanted to tell me. No one thought that I would want to know my biological father, or the story of heartbreak, or who I was and where I came from. The nose on my face that was so vastly different from those of my siblings, my lack of height, my emotional demeanor, and the constant sensation that I was somehow different—all of these observations, differences that I had felt guilty about noticing for years— was valid. I hadn't been imagining things. I was not crazy.

But I was heartbroken. Not only had I just lost my mother, I now had to mourn losing my father Tom *as* my father as well. Tom was not my father. Oh my God. Had *he* known all along? And what about Tommy, Susie, and Dale? The sudden realization that they weren't my full siblings anymore made me feel even more alone.

All those years, they knew. All the times I joked at the dinner table that I must have been the milkman's child; the times I asked why our parents had divorced; the time I wondered why I was so much shorter, so much darker, so much more emotional, they knew (or suspected). And said nothing.

I couldn't drive anymore. My tears were obscuring the lines on the road, and I knew I was becoming a danger to myself and to others. I pulled over in front of some stranger's desert cactus garden and parked.

I called my husband. When he answered, I started to tell the story, but words wouldn't form. Instead, from my mouth came unearthly sounds. Howls. The cries of a wounded animal. I sobbed, and David was speechless at my pain, assuming it came from the death of my mother and not knowing what to do or what to say to calm me.

When I finally squeaked out the true story—my discovery of betrayal and of the secrets that had been kept by so many for years—after his shock died down enough to speak, after countless confused utterances of "Oh My God" and "They said what?", he sighed heavily and said, "You have to forgive your mother. Let her spirit know that you do. It's important."

"But I'm not angry with her," I said, and I wasn't. I was angry at everyone else. I felt an instant surge of empathy for my mother. In a flash, I suddenly understood her lifelong melancholy, her frantic avoidance of details, the muffled sobs from her bedroom.

"No, it must have been horrible for her, having to keep this secret."

"Tell her you forgive her anyway. Her soul needs to know this."

The thought of my mother in some sort of floating purgatory, looking down and knowing the pain she had caused me, broke me. I was protecting her still.

So, after I hung up with David, I did it. It wasn't convincing, but I whispered, "I forgive you, Mama," into the Arizona sunset.

I got silence in return.

Well. Why would she be any different in death than she was in life?

I couldn't go back to the house in Green Valley, so I kept driving north to Tucson and The Folk Shop. The kantele was gone, and so was the six-string ukulele I had decided to buy as an ironic consolation for discovering I was a bastard child. The store seemed small and dirty, and I didn't get the feelings of wonder and serenity I had when I was there just the previous week. I cried in the banjo room, which is a metaphor in and of itself. I got back into the car and drove aimlessly until Dale texted.

Are you all right? We're getting worried about you.

I waited a few minutes before I texted back. A part of me wanted to make them nervous, make them think that I wasn't coming home. I wanted payback. The very least I could give them was a few more minutes of worry. But there weren't enough minutes to make up for fifty-one years of omissions, so I simply texted, *I'm on my way back.*

Time to face the music and go back to Green Valley. I knew what I had to do next.

Hello, Google...

CHAPTER THIRTY-TWO

THE SHADOW MAN

T his is what I knew for sure about my presumed biological father:

1. His name: Donald Garnett.
2. He lived in or around Delaware at the time of my birth. The paper upon which he chose to profess his everlasting devotion to my mother was engineering computation paper with the DuPont logo stamped on the bottom of the page, which meant I could assume that...
3. He worked for DuPont.

And that was all. I knew three details about my father, and I wasn't even one-hundred percent sure about his name. Dale's memory could be incorrect. After all, it had been fifty years since I was born. But, it was a place to start, so I typed "Donald Garnett, Delaware" into the Google search engine, closed my eyes, and pushed return.

The very first listing made me gasp. I stared at the computer without breathing for what felt like an hour, the real world dissolving around me. Staring back at me was the picture of a very old man, with eyes so kind and sad. Eyes that said, "I'm sorry this is the way we had to meet." My nose perched on his ancient face, my nasal labial folds, my smile. If I were an old man, this is what I would look like.

The picture was listed with an obituary from a funeral home in Colorado. The obituary was sparse and revealed little detail, but the picture...

Recognition. A deep instinctual knowing.

I knew immediately: *This* was my father.

I pondered the date of his death: March 1, 2016. Not in the early '70s from a heart attack as my mother had told me the day I asked about the man in the photo. If this internet Don was indeed my father, he died only a year and a half ago. With sudden heart-sinking revelation, I realized I could have had a father for all these empty years. My daughters could have known their grandfather. I could have had someone walk with me down the aisle when I married. If this Don Garnett was my father, I would *never* have the chance to meet him, to ask if he loved me, to hear the story of the love affair with Ernie from his own mouth. I stared at his picture while the world swirled around me, wondering how on earth this all could be true, and if I had indeed found my biological father on the first hit of a Google search.

Just in case my instinct was wrong (how I love to second guess myself), I continued my search for other Don Garnetts across the country, but I knew in my heart I had already found my man. My Father. Now, I needed proof.

I couldn't sleep that night. The couch was already too short and uncomfortable, and I dreamt of my mother's soul hiding in her open, gaping mouth, waiting to be released, knowing her secret was still untold. I dreamt of my father's eyes staring back at me from the computer, and every time I awoke from these nightmares, I felt the heartbreak wash over me anew. I was haunted by my mother's death and the betrayal of keeping the truth about my father from me, a father it was too late to ever know.

In the morning, sick with sleeplessness and grief but fired up with the strength and certainty of the innocent wronged, I knew I had one more uncomfortable, nearly impossible task to tackle: Jim. Did he know too?

How do you casually ask the man you've been consciously trying to avoid for forty-three years the most personal, gut-wrenching question you possibly could? I had been hiding, protecting myself and my emotions from him for so long, constantly curled up like a hedgehog, shielding my soft middle. Asking meant revealing my vulnerability, opening up that little door that I had slammed shut the day my stuffed kittens were locked in a cage, and double bolted the day my husky boy jeans were paraded around the living room. My mother's death had blown that door wide open and left it hanging unhinged. I would never be able to shut it again.

There was also an unexpected and unwelcome part of me that was worried about Jim. He was so broken. Erni had been his wife for forty-three years, and his pain in losing her was as palpable as my own. If she hadn't told him about Don, would I be destroying his image of her? Would I be throwing gasoline on an already blazing wildfire?

But, by now, you must have an inkling of what I would do. You know there was no way for me *not* to ask. I am not built to hold secrets. I had to pretend to be brave. There was no other option.

I waited until Dale was out on an errand and Susie was walking the golf course, and then I cornered Jim. I could barely speak to him in complete sentences before my mother died, so how on earth would I do this?

I walked into his bedroom where he sat at the computer, organizing my mother's medical bills. Everything must be in its place even when his world has collapsed around him.

Don't cry. Don't cry, Cory. Do NOT cry. Stay cool. I stood in the middle of the room, unanchored, and without segue, I blurted out:

"So, Jim, what do you know about Don Garnett?"

Okay. A little guarded but not defensive. Also, way out of left field.

"I don't know anyone named Don Garnett," he said, but his eyes hold panic and he won't look directly at me. Lies have a certain cadence to them, much different from the songs of omission. In that moment, I knew.

"You're lying." And I lost it. I tried to stop crying. I tried to not reveal myself or my emotions, but I was too broken to hold anything in. The levee had been breached.

And Jim, my stepfather who barely tolerated me for the past forty-three years, started to cry too. Then he did the impossible. He hugged me.

"I would have taken your mother's secret to the grave."

That's the problem, isn't it. They all would have. Everyone protected Erni(e). And everyone thought that by protecting Ernie, they were protecting me.

But they were wrong.

Jim confessed what he knew. The stories he shared were sketchy, and I know there are details he omitted, some that I learned about later and others that he will never tell, but he began with the story of how he met my mother.

Jim sat nursing a beer in a bar in Delaware in 1973 while he was on a business trip for Chrysler. He had sworn off women, being embroiled in the midst of a bitter divorce from his wife, Hortense, but my mother sat at the end of the bar with her friends, Marge and Dottie. Ernie was the most beautiful woman he had ever seen, and he was drawn to her impossible blinding light like a bug to a lantern. After their courtship began, she confided her tale of woe: her affair with Don, the fights with Tom, and her secret love child who knew nothing of the circumstances of her birth.

Maybe she needed to be absolved. Maybe she needed Jim to see her as her true self before they got involved. Maybe she was tired of covering up the truth and lying. Maybe she needed a reason to run away from the gossip in the tight-knit Hercules/Dupont circle, and maybe she believed that in making herself vulnerable through divulging the whole of her situation, Jim would perhaps take pity on her plight and rescue her. I don't know. If that was what she wanted, it worked.

I pressed Jim for more details and he tried to avoid the questions, uncomfortable with both my emotions and his own. With tenacious prodding, which I am annoyingly good at, Jim finally revealed what my mother told him that night in Delaware: Don and Ernie met in an art class (my mother took an art class?!). Tom knew all about their affair and had followed them to and caught them in various hotels. Despite this, Tom told her he didn't care about her affair and she could continue it as long as she never brought Don into the home they shared. Tom had his own romantic extramarital relationships, so perhaps he had a bit of guilt to assuage.

Tom knew whose child I was, and after my birth, he insisted my mother have her tubes tied so he would not have to play father to any other illegitimate children. Ernie agreed that Tom would continue to be known as my father if he would support me financially through college. They also agreed to stay married (at least until Jim came along and cracked that agreement wide open), but Jim had no idea why the relationship with Don ended. During the first few years of my life, my mother had taken me along on trips to visit my biological father. She insisted that it was important for my (real) father to know me. That family was important. The three of us had vacationed together in Quebec and Niagara Falls and the Finger Lakes. Wait. Stop. I knew him. I KNEW him when I was very young. But I cannot remember him now. The Shadow Man. The Hotel Room. The adjoining doors. The fountain. My memory was real. But it is still so frustratingly vague.

Even though Tom and Ernie had come to an agreement about their separate relationships, something must have happened to make them change their minds. Tom had connections within Dupont, and a few well-placed whispers ensured that Don would be transferred out of state, away from me and my mother. "Don had a heart attack and died before I met your mother." Jim said, and I shook my head.

"No. He died in 2016. I found his obituary. I know it's him."

Jim looked shaken. She'd lied to him, too. Or maybe he was lying to me in that moment. At the time, I wasn't sure which was true, but now I know. Jim was lying to me. He knew exactly when Don died—in 2016—because my mother told him. I have no idea who had told her.

Jim asked how I had learned about Don, and I told him about the pictures and the conversation with Dale and Susie on the living room floor the day before.

"Why did your brother and sister tell you this now?" Jim shook his head with sadness and disbelief. For the first time in my life, we agreed on something.

CHAPTER THIRTY-THREE

99.4739%

October 2017

My flight home to Chicago left in the evening from Phoenix. Dale, Susie, and I drove the hour and half north in near silence, each lost in our own reverie. In some ways we were bound closer together than we had ever been before, having gone through the trauma of our mother's death. Trauma has a way of doing that. But, in other ways, we were ripped further apart. I felt a difference, a distance even greater than the one I'd felt before. Something was between us now, or maybe it had always been there and I hadn't been able to see. Like a glass barrier that was once invisible but over time dust and water drops revealed it—my mother was no longer there to ensure it was kept spotlessly clean and transparent. Or, like clouds obscuring the sun; the wavelengths of light hitting the water vapor and scattering the light waves into particles.

We left several hours early for the airport. We all felt the house in Green Valley closing around us like a tomb, so we decided to spend a few hours at the Musical Instrument

Museum in Phoenix. It was my type of outing, learning about the developmental history of folk instruments from all over the world. The three of us wandered around the virtual world listening to samples of drums and stringed instruments, hearing a pulse of rhythm that was the heartbeat of humanity. I thought of my mother's early musical career, and of my own. I thought of My Great Aunt Grace, the opera singer. My daughter Celia Grace is named after her and I realized with a start that she wasn't really my blood relative, as she was Tom's mother's sister. Around every corner was another little death to mourn.

As we wandered through the museum displays, Dale, Susie, and I talked and joked as siblings do, anything to avoid remembering the events of the week. We were all too aware of how brutally grief would envelop us once we were home again, away from this temporary family cocoon. There was comfort in being together for the moment, and there was comfort in the familiar for me—music. I stood in wonder before Sara Carter's autoharp and AP Carter's guitar. I saw my friend, country musician Will Smith, on a museum sponsored video playing the autoharp, and I thought how small the world is, to see someone I know in a museum in Phoenix after my world collapsed.

In order to distract my weary mind on the plane ride home, I opened the book Mama gave me three days before my birthday, *The House at Riverton*. As soon as I finished the first chapter, I skimmed straight to the end because I immediately guessed the "surprise ending" she was so insistent I would enjoy. The book was about a maid who worked at a manor house, and the denouement made it clear that the Lord of the Manor had secretly fathered the heroine.

I roared with laughter. This was how she tried to tell me. Only I didn't bother to read past the first page until after she died.

I fretted over whether or not to tell my daughters about my new family status. David begged me not to burden them; they were already so broken up over their nana's death. He didn't think they needed more baggage, but I knew I could not continue the legacy of secrets and lies. My pain was so great, even larger than the monumental pain of losing a mother, and I thought it was important they understand why I was falling apart. The truth. We must always tell the truth. Wasn't my hidden story proof of that?

Sure enough, as soon as Celia walked into my bedroom the next day after school, I knew I couldn't hide. I sat on the edge of my bed and told her the whole story. Her already huge eyes grew even wider with shock. I knew she wouldn't think differently of my mother, empathetic soul that she is, but I could feel her heart hurting for me. "Oh, Mama. Is there anything I can do for you?" she asked as she hugged me. I shook my head, knowing there was no way to lift this burden, but understanding she needed a task to feel she was doing something for me. Service is her love language.

"You could help me research my family."

"Sure, Mama, I'll do anything to help you."

Celia became my Google Guru, helping me to search for Garnetts, looking for phone numbers and emails and social media accounts. It helped to know that I had a research buddy, that I was not completely alone.

Try as we might, we could not find any other information that would confirm if the man from the Colorado obituary was the same Don Garnett who fathered me. I'd have to turn to his family. I was very hesitant to contact this Don's wife, Dixie, for a number of reasons. The possibility of rejection was painfully real, and I had no desire to tear this woman or her family's life apart if she had no knowledge of my existence. My one consolation was the discovery that Dixie and Don had not married until 1974, well after my birth, so at the very least this wasn't the wife who had come begging to our house on Hercules Road. That woman would have every reason to revile my mother and me. But Dixie might not have a jealous bias against me.

The obituary mentioned that Donald and Dixie had one son named Lee. I thought perhaps I might have less chance of rejection with him—someone born into a younger, more open generation. Lee might be less likely destroyed by the news of his father's secret love child than Dixie, so I turned my search from Donald to his son, looking for a phone number or email address. Try as I might, I found little information about Lee Garnett—which was odd for a man born in the digital era. No cell phone, no social media accounts. No Facebook or Instagram or YouTube videos—none that I could find, at least. I was desperate to see what Don Garnett's son looked like. Did we share a resemblance? Would he be able to identify the man in the pictures as his father?

I did not trust any of the paid online search sites, and hiring a private investigator seemed invasive and dirty, so I refused to go that route. I endlessly and obsessively Googled variations of his name connected to cities that this particular Don Garnett had lived in, but still I found no concrete evidence or contact information. Two weeks after my mother's death, frustrated and at a standstill for proof, I impulsively reached out to the funeral home, hoping

that they could help connect me to the family of Donald I.
Garnett, my Maybe Daddy.

To the Moser Funeral Home:
Hi there, I am a family friend of Donald Garnett and I
am interested in contacting the family to express my sorrow
at his death. Could you pass along their contact information?
Cory Goodrich

I resisted saying, "Hey, I'm Don's illegitimate kid. Can
you hook me up with my new fam?"

Cory,
I am sorry that we are not able to give out any of the
family's information, but I will pass your name and number
on to them so that they can get in touch with you.
Thanks.

I anticipated a reluctance to share the family's contact
info, so I thanked him and said I would appreciate him
passing my email along.

And then I waited, slightly panicked that I had done the
wrong thing. How would Dixie react to this ghost from her
husband's past? What if the news that a child born from an
affair with a married woman was a shock and too much for
her to bear? What if it destroyed her image of her husband?
What if this son, Lee, was uber conservative or thought I
was looking for inheritance money or to stir up trouble? I
hated the thought of hurting anyone and I was very aware
that I could be a most unwelcome surprise.

A bastard.

Illegitimate.

Unwanted.

But I was also churned up with all of the unknowns. Who was I if I was not Tom Goodrich's daughter? Where did I come from? How did I have the same nose as a stranger? What was my medical history? Did I have risks of inherited genetic disease? Did my children? How much of my temperament, my talent, my appearance came from my biological father? And how much of who I am was thanks to Nature rather than Nurture?

There was no way for me not to ask. Not knowing the details was unbearable, unthinkable. It was killing me.

So, I waited. Anxious and heartsick, but determined to find answers.

Two days later an email from Lee arrived in my inbox while I was waiting to pick my daughter up from school, and my heart pounded so hard it could have burst a hole through my chest and fallen onto the ground. I stared at his name and whispered *ohmygodohmygodohmygod* aloud. My hands shook from the reverberation of my pounding heart as I clicked on the email:

October 24, 2:10pm, via email

> *Hi Cory:*
> *My name is Lee Garnett, I'm Donald Garnett's son. We just received word from the funeral home in Colorado about your inquiry. What could I do for you?*
> *Cordially,*
> *Lee*

What do I say? What do I say? I pulled into the garage, threw the car in park (barely), and ran into the house and to my computer to compose this thoroughly inarticulate response:

October 24, 3:04 pm

> *Hi Lee.*
>
> *Thank you so much for getting back to me. First, let me offer my condolences on the passing of your father. My mother, Ernestine, passed away on October 12th and after going through her correspondence and photos, I am looking to find a close friend of hers, and I believe it may be your dad, Don Garnett.*
>
> *I have two photographs that I was hoping you might look at to confirm whether or not this is your father. I know this man would have worked at Dupont in Delaware around 1966. I found a letter to my mother from him written on Engineering Computation paper, so I'm pretty sure about that detail. Would you mind taking a peek and seeing if this might be a photo of your Don Garnett? It's dated June of 1967.*
>
> *I know this is an odd request, and I appreciate your taking the time to help me piece this all together.*
>
> *Cory Goodrich*

I attached one of the two photos to the email, but not the photo's entirety. I figured the image of his father holding a child would be a dead giveaway of whom I was presuming to be. I didn't want to frighten Lee off, so I cropped baby Cory out of the picture but left one chubby baby hand. It was a clue. A breadcrumb. If Lee looked closely, he would know exactly who I was and what I was asking.

October 24, 4:47 pm

I'm very sorry to hear that Cory. Having been through that same disconsolate experience...
(Disconsolate experience...ohmigod, I love him already.)
...Having been through that same disconsolate experience so recently I shouldn't be so bereft for good words of condolence. Maybe there just aren't any which are sufficient for losing a parent.

The photos resemble Pop to me very much. There are some differences, but I haven't seen any photographs of him from this period before. If you'd be willing to forward the letter, I could probably identify his handwriting. It's quite distinctive.

I'd love to hear more about you and your mother on the phone. Perhaps tomorrow? I'm in France, so we'd need to coordinate a time when we both have some daylight.

Lee

He was in France? Why? This was so intriguing. I knew I shouldn't send the entire letter, so I took a photo of the first page, which was not so personal in content, and of the envelope to show the postmark stamped Wilmington, DE.

October 24, 5:09 pm

Hi Lee,
There really are no good words for losing a parent, are there? I was lucky enough to have her until she was almost ninety, so I am taking comfort in the fact she lived a good, long life.

As for the letter, it is quite long, but I will take some
screen shots for you so maybe you will be able to tell some-
thing from that. Whether or not this letter actually belongs
to the man in these pictures is also uncertain to me. They
could totally belong to someone else. Unfortunately, our
parents are not alive to confirm their identity.

Thanks for being open to talking about this. There are
some missing elements to this story, but I believe I have
pieced together a pretty clear narrative, which I will be
happy to share with you tomorrow. Letter pics to follow...
Cory

I was jumbled and frightened, but I pushed Send before I
could edit my clumsy response. If I thought too much about it,
I would chicken out. We agreed to talk the next day at 11am.

Needless to say, I was a hot freaking mess the next
morning, waiting for the call from the son of the man who
might or might not be my father. How would Lee take the
arrival of a secret sister? Was I being foolish for going
down this path no one else wanted me to wander? If Mama
had wanted me to know my father or be a part of another
family, she would have told me, wouldn't she? Maybe this
was wrong, wrong, wrong.

When the phone finally buzzed, I jumped, but I waited
until the third ring to answer, trying to make it appear I
wasn't too eager. I was chill, no need to rush for the phone.
I wasn't nervous at all...

...but my voice squeaked when I said hello. So much
for cool.

"Hello, Cory, this is Lee."

He sounded formal and exotic, with a hint of an untraceable accent. European? Fake? I wasn't sure.

After casual pleasantries neither one of us was interested in, I recounted the story as I knew it so far—what I had pieced together and what I'd made guesses about; where I thought they had met; how I had found the pictures. I told him I suspected Tom had been responsible for Don's transfer somewhere down South, and Lee confirmed Don had indeed been transferred to the Houston plant in the early '70s. I continued rambling about all my suspicions and suppositions, and Lee didn't stop me until I had presented the entire narrative, had bared my soul and my fears and my confusion and confessed all of my desperate Google sleuthing to find my birth father. His silence made me think he was untrusting or in disbelief, and when I finally finished my story, he pressed for clarification on certain details: What did the full letter say? Where did Tom work? Why had no one told me until now? With every question, his voice shook with nerves or emotion. I wasn't sure which, but at least I knew I wasn't alone.

As I answered each query, I realized Lee wasn't asking questions in order to disprove my theories but because he wanted to hear more. He believed me. He was as moved as I by this story of my parents' forbidden love and their secret child. I heard him trying to hold back emotions that were threatening to overwhelm him. How do you process that you have had a secret sister your whole life and never had the chance to know her? To grow up with her? To confide in and argue with her? To share Christmases and birthdays and (especially) funerals with? The momentousness of this conversation, this phone meeting loomed over us both. Who we were to each other had not yet been declared.

"If this is true, Lee, then you are my brother."

"Yes, and you would be my lost sister. I always wanted a sister." There was silence on both ends of the line. All we had missed. All that had been kept from us. All the time lost. There were no words to capture that feeling.

Lee continued, "And you would also have two other siblings: Pop's children from his first marriage to Liz."

I don't know why this hit me so hard, but it did. As heavy as the Acme anvil that the Road Runner dropped on poor Wile E. Coyote's cartoon head. His first marriage. Liz must have been the wife who came to my mother's house, pleading to save her marriage. Three new siblings. I used to be the youngest of four, now I was one of seven. These other two children must have been in the picture while my mother and my father were having a relationship. What scars did they carry from the unwanted love affair between Don and Ernie? Would they blame me for my existence?

"You know, Lee, I don't judge my mother and your father for what they did—for the affair. People do crazy things when they are in love. I hope this doesn't alter your opinion of him."

He sniffed and dismissed my concern. "Are you kidding me? I think adultery is the most beautiful form of love. I'm a bit jealous of you, actually. I wish I were born of an affair."

It was a surprising thing to say. How could anyone be jealous of this? I was a disaster, the cause of my parents' divorce, a love child. But in that moment Lee did what he continues to do to this day. He peered inside my heart and saw my deepest fears and mortifications and washed them away. Normalized them. Normalized me. He wasn't ashamed of his father. And he wasn't ashamed of me, either.

In fact, Lee was grateful and thanked me for searching so diligently. He told me how courageous I was to reach out to him. He declared me the Lost Sister Detective Agency, and I was delighted by his turn of phrase, his voice, his openness, his everything. I was sure this was my brother, my blood, and my lost connection.

I also fully anticipated Lee's need for proof, so I wasn't surprised when he asked for full copies of the pictures and the letter, and we agreed to do a DNA test to confirm that we were indeed siblings. As we waited two endless weeks for the results, we traded texts and family photos and stories. He said he didn't need the DNA test; he was sure from the moment he saw my picture that I was his sister, just as I knew with certainty that Don was my father the second I locked eyes on his obituary photograph. If we listen to our intuition, it's usually right. Our intellect is the fucker that mucks up our certainty.

Lee told me the first thing he did when he first received my email was Google me. (Like Sister, like Brother.) He was sitting on his bed in a hotel in France, and the first picture that appeared was my professional headshot. "Oh..." He saw my nose. HIS nose. His father's nose. "Oh my God, I have a sister."

This nose of mine has always been the bane of my existence. It's unlike anyone else's in the family. It's distinctive. Too big, quite frankly. My first boyfriend, Marc Dempsey, told me that if I wanted to be an actress, I'd have to have that prominent nose "done." He was not my boyfriend for long, thank you very much. This nose is not a Goodrich nose (of course it isn't.) It's the Balmer nose. Balmer is the name of my paternal grandmother's family. I have the family nose. A family.

My head was reeling. I look like someone. My father.

On a Saturday night, two weeks after I'd taken the DNA test, while David was out with friends and I was at home with our daughters, I got the call.

"Cory, it's Lee. Are you ready for this?"

I sat on the couch in my music room, waiting for the floor to drop out from under me again. It would fall either from the certainty that we were related or the heartbreak that we weren't. I already loved Lee for his acceptance and wit. To officially have him as a brother would mean confirmation of my parentage, and this unbelievable story would be real. To not have him as a brother would also be devastating because I already felt him growing like a tiny seed of hope burrowed in my soul. Either way, I knew I was going to need that couch. And probably a stiff drink as well.

"According to the DNA test, it is a 99.4739% certainty that we are brother and sister."

Silence.

Laughter.

Incredulity.

How do you react when your worst and best fears are confirmed with one little swab of an innocuous Q-tip?

On one hand, this was proof that Tom was not my biological father. There had still been a glimmer of doubt that I was clinging to. After all, my mother was still married to him when I was conceived, so there was still that small possibility I was conceived in the marriage bed and not the adulterer's.

Crash...

On the other hand, this magnificent, well-spoken,

well-travelled, infinitely amazing and interesting man was my brother, and he held the keys to unlocking the doors of my past.

Fall...

And then I cried epic tears for everything. For my mother. For never getting to meet my biological father. For whatever broken love story had existed between Don and Ernie. For the betrayal of my family for keeping this from me. For the love of a man who accepted me from just a picture on the Internet. It was too much to process, too much to feel. Even now, months later with proof and visits and conversations and keepsakes, I still have to sit down and ground myself. It's so easy to swirl off into space or down the toilet with sadness and elation and belief and disbelief. This story belongs in a Lifetime movie. Or as a country song. It shouldn't belong to me.

But it does. This is now my story.

CHAPTER THIRTY-FOUR

MOURNING

There's only a single step between
all out and all in
Over the threshold
To grief
And you know
(You hope)
Someday
You will step once again
Tentatively
Bravely
Fully
Into the light.
But today
Inside
It's dark
And cold
Marble and steel
And all the socks and sweaters
Won't take the chill from
My heart.

CHAPTER THIRTY-FIVE

EULOGIES

Thanksgiving 2017

I've taken my family back to Arizona for Erni's Celebration of Life. It's not a funeral or a memorial, but a party in her honor. The residents of Green Valley, Arizona, are used to living with death. It becomes a part of their routine, a daily event to check the obituaries to see which neighbors have passed on. They don't want funerals or sad memorials. They want a reason to celebrate because they know their time is coming too, and if they spend their days crying over each friend who has crossed over, Arizona will no longer be a desert. It will be an ocean of tears.

We also wanted to spend Thanksgiving together as a family one last time. My nieces and nephews were there as well as Dale's wife, Stephanie, and Susie's husband, Bill. It was chaotic and there was genuine laughter even though my mother is dead and we were about to have her memorial. It amazes me how hard you can laugh in the midst of mourning. The jokes and stories shared about Mama and our time growing up together were life affirming. It was like nothing happened, and yet we all felt the overwhelming, weighty presence of Erni's absence.

I was nervous because, before we got on the plane, Lee texted me and said he had gotten into a discussion with his...my...our...brother, who disagreed with Lee's decision to tell his mother about me at their Thanksgiving dinner. He believed that telling her would be an act that might only cause her pain.

All of my defenses went up. "I will not be kept a secret again. I'm not something to be ashamed of."

"Of course, you are not. No more lies. I will tell her."

"I'm certain she already knows about me, Lee. That's my instinct."

Lee had been incredible to me and for me. He repeated how much he loves me and how proud he is that I was brave enough to find him. But it doesn't feel like bravery to me. Desperation, maybe. Insanity, definitely.

More than anything, I just needed connection—with my father, with Lee, and with anyone connected to him. I needed an anchor, something to pull me back to earth. Or maybe, what I actually needed was a buoy—something to save me from drowning.

At the Thanksgiving dinner table in Green Valley, I secretly invited Lee to join us. He wasn't there in person; he was in Texas with his mother and their Thanksgiving feast, but he was texting me while we were eating turkey and stuffing. I was half listening to the conversation of my OG's while I talked to my new sibling, iPhone hidden under the table. I felt like I was cheating on the family I grew up with.

But it was so worth it.

Lee told his mother, and he was bursting with information.

"Mom already knew. Said Dad had told her in 1974. She asked if Ernie loved Dad and he said yes, and he loved her as much."

I typed furtively under the dining room table, unbelievably relieved that this news did not take his mother by surprise.

"You were right about Tom's involvement in ending the affair. I remember Pop telling the story of being called in for a meeting with his boss at Dupont, thinking he was getting a promotion but getting transferred instead. What he didn't mention was the reason. Apparently, the company told him they knew all about Ernie. 'This stops now, Garnett, or you will never work in this business again,' and then they transferred him to Houston. Mom confirmed this."

"Ahhhh! Really? What else did she say?"

And this was the moment where my heart shattered into a thousand pieces of glittering, fragmented glass crystals:

"Dad told Mom that your birth was intentional, that Ernie had wanted a child with him, and he wanted it too."

I didn't know until the moment Lee wrote those words how deeply I had been burying the fear that I was an accident, a mistake, something that ruined both of their lives.

But I wasn't.

Ernie wanted a child with Don, he agreed, and I was created out of Love.

I was Intentional. Planned. Wanted.

I was indeed a Love Child.

We held Erni's Celebration of Life on the Friday afternoon after Thanksgiving. Friday was Bridge Day, and Bridge Day is sacred to the retirees of Green Valley. No person or event is important enough to warrant canceling a bridge event. Until now. For the first time in Green Valley history, the Bridge Club cancelled their Friday game so that my mother's fellow players could attend her memorial.

Erni was a brilliant bridge player, and reached the title of Ruby Life Master by the time of her passing. *The Bridge Bulletin* even published her name in their magazine, announcing her death. How often she would beg me to learn to play, but I usually stared at her, glassy eyed, while she explained the game and strategy. Then she would sigh, and we'd play Gin Rummy, which is definitely more my speed.

In lieu of prayer cards, which seemed too religious and formal for a woman who had been kicked out of the church, my niece Caroline created a deck of playing cards with "Erni, Our Queen of Hearts" printed on the back of each card. Different photos from the various stages of my mother's life were printed on the faces. It was the perfect tribute for my mother, the bridge wiz.

Dale acted as master of ceremonies and eulogized about the sunrise he witnessed a few days after her death. He stood on the patio in the dusk before dawn, the moon hanging low on the horizon, a wisp of a crescent, a shallow U. Venus, my mother's ruling planet, or the Morning Star, hung directly below it, and the effect was that of a closed eye with a tear falling gently below it. Even the heavens wept for my mother. I think of my mother's solitary tear, rolling down from her taped eye. This was no coincidence.

Jim, Susie, and a few of Erni's friends gave touching speeches about my mother's kindness, her intelligence, and her compassion. In the middle of Susie's speech, I noticed

Jim gesturing for her to speed up and finish. Susie was distracted by his sign language, trying to figure out why he was passive aggressively interrupting her speech. She faltered. I was mortified, not only for my sister and the people witnessing this tense interaction, but also because I realized that, a year earlier, I would have been the one on the receiving end of Jim's microaggression. Susie and I had switched places. Suddenly I was the golden girl, and she was bearing the brunt of his antagonism.

She had been poised to say something heartfelt about my mother's and Jim's marriage but was so flustered by his flailing that she never said what she had planned. She looked stricken. I could empathize. I knew exactly what that felt like.

I was the last to speak. Deciding what to say to my mother's friends and neighbors had left me in a quandary. I was still swirling, in a complete downward spiral from all the things she had kept from me. How was I supposed to talk about my mother when I felt like I never even knew who she was? Would anything I said even be true? But, when I looked around at all of the faces in the room, at over one hundred and twenty-five retirees, some with tears in their eyes, some having shared beautiful memories of how kind and memorable my mother was to them, I knew what my message should be.

"Life is like a book," I started.

"Every person has a life full of chapters, and you rarely get to read the entire novel of a person's life. You live the pages you're in and if you're lucky, you get a Cliff's notes recap of the paragraphs that came before or after you.

"My mother had so many different chapters in her book

of life. I came into the story somewhere in the middle, and while I know how the novel ends, Part One is a mystery to me because she kept a substantial amount of the words hidden, more like a locked diary than a bestseller.

"She shared 'paragraphs' of her childhood: Stories of her grandfather's mansion where her mother roller-skated in a second-floor empty ballroom; memories of sleeping in the big featherbed that was so tall she had to use a step stool to climb into it; the school dance she attended with her boyfriend, who happened to be in the Navy at the time. His uniform pants had thirteen buttons on the front, representing the thirteen original colonies."

There was a murmur of recognition from many in the audience, as this prompted a collective memory from their World War II generation.

"The gym floor had been freshly waxed," I continued, "and her shoes were brand new and slippery..." I heard a titter. They knew where this story was going. "...so, when she took her first step onto that dance floor, she went down. In an attempt to break her fall, she grabbed for the nearest available thing, which happened to be the waistband of her boyfriend's Navy uniform pants. Thirteen original colony buttons went flying across the room and rolled across the gym floor. My mother went into a fit of laughter when she told that story. I loved to hear her laugh. She was vivacious, and her smile always had a hint of the devil in it." The audience nodded. Her friends knew how impish she could be.

I remembered this story not only because I loved the image of the buttons propelled through the air and coming to a rolling stop between the feet of the students on the dance floor, but because it was one of the *only* stories she had told me about her school years.

When Mama spoke of being a teenager, which was seldom, something came over her. Sadness, a hint of belligerence, quiet resentment. I knew that she had sung with her sisters, but she had never shared the details: travelling to an Air Force base to perform for the troops during a blackout, the road covered by pitch darkness to protect the location of the soldiers; being chosen out of one thousand applicants to sing at the New York World's Fair, which would appear on a telecast from the RCA television studios at the exposition.

What she did always speak of was how her mother had ruined her life by forcing her to take dancing and singing lessons, making her perform instead of doing the things that her schoolmates were allowed to do. How she resented having to perform. And this is why the story of the dance and the flying buttons stuck with me. Maybe it was one of the only "normal" teenage things she had gotten to do. I didn't mention this to the people of Green Valley attending my mother's memorial. Many of them were surprised she had ever been a singer. They had only heard her talk of my career.

I continued. "When I was in high school, the Smiths lived across the street in an old, run-down house. The paint was peeling and the lawn was a foot overgrown, and right in the center of the long grass was the ugliest bright, baby blue birdbath you've ever seen. Our other next-door neighbors, the Johns, complained bitterly about that eyesore. One night, my mother and another neighbor, Alice, got it into their heads that they should steal that bird bath. And just like that, my mother became a cat burglar... (bird burglar?) Around midnight, Alice and Ernie snuck into the Smith's yard, still fully decked out from their evening party, and they carried that birdbath, heels sinking and sticking in the mud, across the street to its new place of honor: smack in the middle of Connie John's front yard.

"My mother denied responsibility, but everyone knew it was her doing. She couldn't stop laughing at the thought of Connie waking up to find her new hot lawn ornament, prominently displayed in her front yard. Both Connie and the Smiths were livid, but no one could stay mad at my mother for long.

"Ernie's act of rebellion was revelatory for me. In my experience, most mothers don't typically steal things, so I was half shocked, half mortified, and totally embarrassed, but I was also incredibly proud. My mom was a badass."

Ok, I didn't actually call her a badass. I don't think that would have gone over well with the octogenarian crowd, but that was what I meant. I admired her mischievous act. The neighbors got their birdbath back (alas), so it wasn't malicious. But it was damned funny.

"Then there was a chapter of her life that revolved around performing. She and her sisters were known as 'The Stairstep Sisters' and 'The Debs of Rhythm.' They were incredibly successful, but she never talked about those years because she hated singing so much. I'm sure Mama noticed the irony of my wanting to be an actress.

"My mother would come to see many of my shows in Chicago, and as we drove home from the theatre after a performance, she would tell me what she thought of each actor; who was talented and who was just so-so. But she never commented on my performance, neither praise nor critique. It drove me nuts. She'd talk about everything else

BUT me. Finally, on one post-show drive, after listening to her give her review I snapped at her. 'Why don't you ever tell me you liked MY performance?' And, a bit shocked and taken aback, she said, 'because I just assumed you knew that I ALWAYS think you are wonderful.' That's just how she was. She just assumed you knew she loved you or loved your work. She didn't say the words, but you KNEW. Or you were supposed to anyway."

Truth be told, I never really understood just how much she loved me, or that I was special to her. Not until I realized how desperately she had tried to protect me. Not until this moment in front of a room full of her friends. Friends who heard her speak endlessly of her daughter, the actress. Friends who knew almost everything about me. I could see it in their eyes as they listened to my words. I faltered, hoping I hadn't sounded bitter in front of the people who loved her. I continued.

"Ironically, it wasn't until I started writing my own music that something shifted with Mama. Suddenly, she started telling me how much she liked my songs or the lyrics I wrote, or that she liked the way my voice sounded when I sang country music. When it came to the things that were true to ME, that I wrote and created, she became enthusiastic about telling me how much she approved. She wanted to hear MY story, MY words. And she also thought every song I wrote should be on the radio. And of course, she was right." The audience laughed.

"If I have one thing to leave you with today it's this: Let people read your book. Tell them your stories, read the chapters aloud, even if they don't seem to be listening. Share who you are, because someday your words are going to mean the world to someone who didn't get to read the whole opus of your life. I'm not sure if my mother was a romance novel, or a mystery, or a western, but I'm grateful I got to be a character of her story." I was probably the antagonist.

Before my mother's surgery, I asked what her favorite song was, and she answered immediately, "Tumbling Tumbleweeds." Maybe the three-part harmony of the Sons of the Pioneers reminded her of singing with her sisters, or maybe the languid loneliness and the image of a cowboy alone under the stars contemplating his life drew her to this song.

I grabbed my ukulele, and Susie, her oldest daughter Heather, and I sang in three-part harmony...just as Ernie used to sing with her sisters.

See them tumbling down
Pledging their love to the ground!
Lonely, but free, I'll be found
Drifting along with the tumblin' tumbleweeds
Cares of the past are behind
Nowhere to go, but I'll find
Just where the trail will wind
Drifting along with the tumblin' tumbleweeds
I know when night has gone
That a new world's born at dawn!
I'll keep rolling along
Deep in my heart is a song
Here on the range I belong
Drifting along with the tumbling tumbleweeds.

After our performance, we had a good old-fashioned square dance in the common room of the rec center. Mama would have loved it. Just as she could never get me to play bridge, she could never get me to a square dance. She seemed to be working her magic from the afterlife to get me to do one on this day.

As people were leaving the memorial, close friends shared their own stories about "Erni with an 'i'." She was so well loved. One of her closest friends, Roberta, stopped me as I was cleaning up a tray of sandwiches. There were tears in her eyes as she told me she and my mother shared their natal day. They were birthday twins. What will she do without her, she wondered?

"Cory, I know you said she never complimented you on your performances, but she talked about how wonderful you are all the time."

"Did she? We fought constantly you know. I think I drove her crazy."

Roberta looked at me quizzically. "When I think of the quintessential mother/daughter relationship, I think of Erni and how she felt about you. She may not have told you because she wanted you to stay grounded, but I have never seen a mother prouder of her child." Roberta looked at me pointedly. "You were very special to her."

I wondered if she knew my mother's secret. I couldn't ask. I was so torn up inside, missing my mother, confounded by why she had kept the truth of my father from me, but I was also unwilling to destroy the image she had worked so hard to maintain with one of her closest friends.

I knew my mother, but I didn't, just as I thought I had known who I was, and suddenly found I didn't know that either.

That evening, Dale, Susie, and I stood outside the house in Green Valley, looking up at the stars, wondering if our mother was now one of them. We were completely irreverent the way siblings are when a parent has died and they need to will away the veil of sadness. We laughed when we saw our long shadows on the driveway cast from the front door light. Dale's silhouetted legs looked impossibly long and skinny.

"Look, I'm Tommy Hyatt." We laughed, remembering Mama's wedding photos, and the way her first husband looked stretched out and emaciated, painfully skinny.

"You never know, maybe Tommy Hyatt is my real father," Dale said, and I laughed awkwardly. I appreciated him trying to lighten the mood, to poke fun at my illegitimate status, but it was still a bit too soon. I am still too raw for jokes like that.

I will always be too raw for jokes like that.

The three of us and our dark counterparts stood lined up next to each other on the driveway, and the shadow of us looked like a string of paper dolls holding hands. When Tommy came outside to join us, wondering why the three of us were laughing in the driveway, we started to bicker about something, as we usually seem to do when the four of us are all together. Then we fell silent, looking at the Mother Stars and the line of Paper Children. We knew this was quite possibly the last time we would ever all be together again.

CHAPTER THIRTY-SIX

SIGNS

December 2017—Chicago

I've known people who have lost their spouses, parents, siblings, or friends, and so many of them, in their cloud of pain and grief, have spoken to me of seeing signs. Perhaps they found pennies imprinted with their loved one's birth year or feathers on the sidewalk that served as a signal that their loved one was attempting to contact them from the beyond. Truth be told, I always felt a little sorry for these people, to be so lost in their sorrow that they turn ordinary, everyday things into spiritual communiqués. Lost pennies can always be found scattered in the streets, and feathers...well...look up. There are birds everywhere. Those things they take as signs are physical objects that are always present in our earthly world, but the grief-stricken see in them what they want to see: proof that their loved one is not gone after all but instead right there next to them, perhaps in another dimension trying to communicate through the veil by yelling in tiny Who-like voices, "We are here, We are here, We are HERE."

But they are not here. They are gone. I don't know where to, exactly, or if there is a heaven or an afterlife, but I look at those symbols as more of a manifestation of our own refusal to let go; we need to believe that our husband or mother or child has not just vanished—disappeared leaving nothing more than a sense memory of their hand pressed in yours.

And yet...

My husband, David, sees hawks.

He began to notice them shortly after his father died, and he took it as a portent from his now heavenly father that Joe was still here with him, in spirit. After a while, I started seeing them too, and even though I didn't receive the hawks as a physical manifestation of Joe Barron, I did acknowledge them as a message for me to stop and take note, to remember my father-in-law and say a prayer for him.

After my mother died, I started ruminating on these messages from the want-to-be beyond, and I was determined not to turn ordinary events into imagined signs that she was communicating with me. Like my hawk sightings, I would take them as reminders from my higher self to stop and think of her, not as a firm belief that any ghosts were looking to hook-up and say *heyyyyyy*.

When the manager in my local grocery store started flirting with me, I joked (and it was a joke, not wishful thinking) that it was my mother sending a sign. Mama was always so tickled that whenever I went to the Safeway in Green Valley, an older gentleman, presumably looking for a new young wife, would make eyes at me in the cereal aisle over the All-Bran or offer to buy my groceries because I was such a lovely young thing and needed to be taken care of. My mother was proud that her daughter had the same allure to men that she once had. So, after the grocery store manager made eyes at me while restocking the frozen vegetables a week after my mother's death, I joked on social media that it was a message from her, and a multitude of people commented, "YES! The signs are there if you are open to them!" I politely agreed and thanked them for explaining it to me, but inside I was like, *suckers.*

And then the hawk appeared.

Not in the sky, circling, looking for a rabbit, something I would naturally see on any mid-morning walk if I just looked up, but in my very own backyard. And not just in my backyard, but on the railing of my deck. A foot from the house. In plain view from my window as I sat writing.

Hi, Mama.

David laughed and said, "So you don't believe in signs, do you?"

Ok, maybe. Maaaaybeeee, but, really...it's just a bird. Birds land on the deck, it's not that unusual—even though we have never before seen a hawk in our yard let alone on our back deck, so up close and personal.

And then one morning a few days later, as I worked at the computer writing about Erni(e), I looked up and saw the Christmas tree lights flash on and off. I remarked to David that perhaps it was her checking in. "Mama, if that's you, make the lights flash again!" Nothing happened. "See!? Not a sign from the beyond." My cynicism was validated, and as I smugly chuckled and turned back to my work, I glanced out the bay window into my backyard. At that very moment, the hawk flew down and landed on the birdbath, turned to throw a very pointed glare at me over its left wing, and flew off again.

We see what we want to see. We ascribe meaning to ordinary events, but maybe that's the point. Maybe the ordinary isn't ordinary at all. Maybe it doesn't matter if it is a ghost causing a bulb to short in my Christmas tree or directing a hawk to scold me through my kitchen window. Maybe *everything* is a sign, a symbol, or a portent, and we just need someone or something to open our eyes to the extraordinary meaning in every little moment.

CHAPTER THIRTY-SEVEN

MARGINAL

She writes in the margins
Of poems
And books
And things she likes.
She writes dates
And parentheses,
Of things remembered
And love expressed.
She shares a deep connection
With the one who wrote
The words.
She writes in the margins
But never tells me
I am loved
Or not my father's child.
She wants you to guess
The secrets
By her dates
And circles
And things remembered.
She has written in my margins
But I don't know the language
Of the markings of her past.
And I forgot to ask the questions
Before the ink had dried.

CHAPTER THIRTY-EIGHT

IVY (AKA THE WHOLE F@&%ING WORLD)

Wilmington, Delaware, 1970

We met on my first day of kindergarten. That morning, my mother walked me to the end of our long asphalt driveway, and I climbed happily onto a big yellow bus that took me to Marbrook Elementary School and my waiting teacher. Several hours later, I was back on the bus, and I was terrified. How could the bus driver possibly remember where I lived? What if he drove right past my long driveway? I was convinced I was lost to my family forever, and I would never again sleep in my bedroom with the pink gingham curtains and my basket of stuffed kittens. I sat on the sticky, blue, vinyl bus seat crying softly, hoping no one would notice my anxiety.

But a girl seated behind me did notice.

"Hey, you want me to come sit with you?"

I turned and surveyed her. She had brown, straight hair cut into a Buster Brown bob, and it had clearly not seen a hairbrush that morning. Fascinating brown freckles covered her cheeks and pug nose. Fearless brown eyes stared quizzically at me, curious as to why I was crying.

"You can't come sit with me." I replied. "The bus is moving, and we're not allowed to change seats." I was upset, but I was not going to get in trouble on top of things. I was not a rule breaker. I heard enough yelling at home; I did not want to be yelled at by the bus driver too.

"They won't see me," she said confidently, and she slid to the filthy floor of the bus and crawled under two bench seats to get to me. I was horrified. And thrilled.

"Ivy Lynn, get back in your seat!"

I don't know how the bus driver knew her name on the first day of school, but her reputation somehow already preceded her. Already known as the troublemaker of Westminster Park, she was only five years old, and that daring crawl under the bus seats set the tone for our entire relationship. We would be naughty and Ivy would get busted, but I would not, even though I was fully involved with whatever crazy scheme we had cooked up. I was a good girl, and I must have been poorly influenced by the imp with the bad home life and horrible reputation. We were C.C. Bloom and Hillary Whitney, Thelma and Louise, Laverne and Shirley.

We were an odd match, but we were also inseparable. Ivy was a fierce friend over the years. She stood up for me when Tom/my dad did something she deemed inappropriate, like neglecting to hang a mirror in my bare bones post-divorce teenage bedroom. The next day, a mirror would miraculously appear. Her loyalty was a boon, but I began to find it strangely oppressive as we grew. She was controlling, and she treated me like I was precious, and I hate being treated that way. Our summers were filled with arguments and contrition. Nevertheless, she was my best friend. And she was my only friend in Delaware.

She loved my dad, and he accepted her as one of his own, which was apparently a specialty of his; he was a collector of strays and lost things. She was a constant fixture at our house in the summers; in the basement playing submarine with me in the toy chest; on the swings where we would pretend we were on African safaris; at the country club pool where she was not a member but wore a stolen member's badge so that we could swim together. She was as much a part of my summers as Daddy and the giant Hershey bars and the mini bottles of Coke.

She also hated my mother. I mean, really loathed her.

Ivy would tear into her ruthlessly, saying she broke my father's heart by divorcing him. She said Ernie was a bad mother, the name Ernie spoken with palpable venom and distaste. This caused an unbreachable rift between us. After all, my mother was still my mother. I loved her, and I simply could not understand this vitriol against her. I would ask Ivy to lay off, but her malicious comments always returned. We'd "break up," and each of us would sit home alone, sometimes for several precious summer weeks, waiting until the other caved and apologized. But in the end, we always made up because I didn't have any other friends left in Delaware, and she didn't have many either. I was lonely and I needed her. She needed me and my father.

In the winter months when I was back in Michigan, Ivy would continue to visit Daddy. It was odd, but strangely comforting to know they hung out together when I was gone. Years later, while I was in college, Daddy walked into the house, having returned from a round of golf, and he caught Ivy stealing money from the top drawer of his yellow dresser. She told him she needed the money because she was pregnant. Rather than call the police, Daddy asked, "How much?" and gave her the cash as a loan. He never expected to get all of the money back, but she broke his heart when she didn't even try, didn't make a single effort to repay him. Even five dollars would have been an act of faith, but, for whatever reason, she wouldn't—or couldn't—do it.

I had difficulty forgiving her, and it wasn't her act of thievery that caused that. After all, my dad had chosen not only to forgive her but to help her. Even after he died and she refused to settle the "loan" with my father's estate, it wasn't about the money. It was that she had the audacity to hate my mother for breaking my father's heart, and yet she, for very different reasons, betrayed his trust and hurt him too. We broke ties after that, and I didn't speak to her for twenty-five years.

One morning in January, three months after my mother died, I was getting ready for work, simultaneously obsessing over the bad country song that was my life. From out of the clear blue, like a lightning bolt and every other cliché you can imagine, an intuition struck me. I literally looked at my face in the mirror and said out loud, "Ivy. She knows." The sudden realization surprised me, but I was sure of it.

I ran downstairs to my computer and sent her a message via Facebook, even though I hadn't spoken with her since 1991, a year after Daddy had died. After a few cryptic DMs, I called her. This really wasn't a conversation to have via text.

"Ivy, what do you know about my parents' divorce?" I left the question purposefully vague.

"I don't know who your real father is—" she blurted out in a panic.

Holy. Shit.

Unbelievable. She knew. Once again, my intuition had nailed it.

"Even if it was idle gossip, tell me what you know."

I expected a bit of hesitation, more concern for my well-being, or a searching through years of dusty memories, but she launched right into the story as if she had been waiting to tell it to me for years. There's a sort of glee some people take in bringing someone down, something that loosens their lips and the allows the words to slide out like poisonous oil.

"Your mother was a slut," Ivy says.

A slut.

I hate that horrible, judgmental word reserved only for woman. Is there a comparable word for a man? If there is, I'm sure it's a badge of honor.

Wild anger rose in my throat and I could barely speak. How dare she. These names that people use to defame others, to label them with scarlet letters, anointing them with hatred and bias. Slut. Bastard. Illegitimate. Adulterer. It's so much easier to fix the lens of judgement on someone else than take a good introspective look in the mirror and see that we are all human beings dealing with our own circumstances in the best way we can.

Ivy continued her pillory of my mother.

"They were swingers. Everyone in the neighborhood knew about that affair. They all talked about her."

"But when did you hear this, Ivy?"

"On the day your moving van pulled away, I sat on the edge of the driveway and cried for hours. My father finally came to get me, and Tom invited us in. He told us everything. He admitted you were not his child. Tom spoke of the affairs he had in retaliation, but in the end, Ernie's leaving broke him. No one approved of your mother. She was a Wild Woman."

Ivy's judgment of Ernie was sharp and stark. Black and white. No forgiveness.

"You know, you were once a Wild Woman too, Ivy"

Silence.

"And why is SHE is labeled a slut when my father admitted to the same behavior?"

More silence.

"How could you possibly know what was in her heart, whether or not she was in love, felt ignored or hopeless? How can you judge what you know absolutely NOTHING about? And what kind of person are you? How can you say such cruel things to me when my mother is not five months in her grave? What kind of person says this to their once best friend? Do you know how ugly and hypocritical your judgement is? How disgusting it is to hear you call my mother such a vile name? How dare you."

I didn't say a single word of this, but I wanted to. I wish I had. It was just like all our childhood breakups but magnified by a million. This time, there will be no making up. I will never speak to Ivy again. Forgiveness is a door that swings both ways, but I have locked that door and melted down the key.

CHAPTER THIRTY-NINE

REVISIONIST HISTORY

December 2017 passed in a haze. I don't remember much about that Christmas or New Year or Valentine's Day. I spent my time crying; or thinking about the past that I couldn't change and crying; or thinking about my father(s) and crying. Mostly I spent it missing my mother. And crying. It was a never-ending, tear filled suck-fest.

I could not comprehend why exactly this was putting me in such a swirling vortex. I mean, on paper, nothing had changed. I wasn't suddenly a pauper or ousted from my home because I was an illegitimate love child. I had missed the opportunity to know my father Donald, but since he wasn't a part of my life since those very early childhood years and I had no clear memories of him, did it really matter?

Nothing had changed. But everything was different.

Nothing and everything...

I started to revisit every moment I could remember of my life and saw it through a different filter. Did they say [fill in the blank] because they knew about my situation? How did my siblings feel about me? Did they treat me differently because they knew? Did Daddy hold himself away from me emotionally because he knew I was not his biological child? Did Nana know? Did she tell Tom about the affair, or encourage my mother to divorce Daddy and go to Michigan with Jim? Did my mom marry Jim because she loved him, or because she wanted to shield me from the inevitable gossip? Maybe she had to move me away before I heard the truth from someone like Ivy. Maybe everyone did think of her as a slut.

And what about Don...did he ever love me? Was he sorry to leave me behind when he was transferred to Houston? Why didn't he and "Ernie with an 'e'" reconcile before she became "Erni with an 'i'"? Was I abandoned by my father, and how much of my constant, melancholy longing was due to the fact that the first man who was supposed to love me was gone? I had intuitively felt his absence, so was this feeling similar to experiencing the death of a father at a very young age without knowing it?

I thought about young Ernestine losing her father Caleb at the age of fourteen from a freak turn of events. One day in 1946, his pancreas inexplicably burst, and he refused to seek treatment right away (just like a man). He died two days later at age forty-seven.

Antoinette and her girls were forced to fend for them-selves. I wonder if Caleb's premature death had left Ernie longing for a father figure or for someone to replace the love she could no longer get from Caleb. It was another sort of abandonment, really, though not an intentional one. Did she choose Tom, eighteen years her senior, because he represented a father figure to her? A father she could no longer have?

And then there was Harry Popejoy, who left his wife and young sons to marry another woman (the redhead). Did this paternal abandonment leave Tom with scars that would later ensure that he, in turn, would *not* abandon a girl who believed she was his daughter?

My mother told me that for the first several years of their marriage, Tom insisted his father died when he was a very young boy. Years later, my mother was shocked to find that Tom had lied. Harry actually died in 1941 (when Tom was thirty) due to complications from syphilis (that damned redhead.) In the early years of my father's life, Harry Popejoy may not have been physically dead, but he was dead to Thomas Popejoy Goodrich.

And then there was my mother, inadvertently telling me that the man in the photograph, my biological father, was dead from a heart attack, when in truth he was very much alive—just dead to her.

Both of my parents were abandoned by their fathers.

How much of who I am was shaped by my own "abandonment," however unintentionally, by Don?' Will I ever again be the person I was before I knew where I came from? Do I want to be?

I lost my mother. I lost my father(s). I've lost myself. Now it's time to find me.

CHAPTER FORTY

DARK ANGEL

January 2018

Ever since Thanksgiving, Lee and I have been com-municating non-stop via text. He sends photos of family members I will never know: Blind Aunt Ermel who was still somehow a painter; O.W. and Averil Garnett, both educators; David "Crick" Garnett who, on the day his son was to be drafted into the army, fainted when he miraculously heard the word "Armistice" shouted excitedly from a throng of people in the streets. Stories of people who are mine and not mine. I belong to their family tree, and yet I feel like a branch that has been grafted onto them. The disconnect bothers me. I need to see my family face to face, to touch Lee's hand and feel some connection to the past that both was and wasn't mine.

When I tell him how desperately I want to see him for real, Lee buys a plane ticket to Chicago. We have (rather rashly) decided that after a two-day visit at my house, we will head to Denver together to visit his father's (OUR fa-

ther's) grave. I am touched that he agreed to take me there, and he is touched that I want to make such a pilgrimage.

After our first surreal meeting in front of the O'Hare Starbucks (all of my most significant life events occur in proximity to coffee), we leave the airport and head toward the restaurant I've chosen. It's a surreal thing, picking a stranger up at the airport and trying to make up for the last forty-one years you've missed. It's even more awkward when that stranger is a blood relative and yet so different from your suburban, whitewashed world. My social circles are not that stodgy—I am in the theatre, after all—but still, it is far more gentrified and boring than I care to admit. Lee is anything but boring.

He's different. He's dark and quiet, and I'm not sure yet if that darkness is grief or danger. Every molecule in me is vibrating with fear and excitement and familiarity. I am not sure where this man will take me or what the end result will be. Will I end up dead in a ditch or finally free of all the darkness that resides so deeply in my heart? For some inexplicable reason I call him Dark Angel in my mind, but I realize now that I am meeting him that maybe he is the White Witch—the one who works magic for good—and I am the Dark Angel. My soul is heavy and troubled.

Dinner is awkward. We don't know how the conversations should start; we don't have the shorthand of siblings who grew up together. The restaurant is noisy, which makes it difficult to talk. David is on painkillers for his back and not as gregarious as usual. I find myself constantly at a loss for words, wondering how to impress this brother I never knew I had. He is incredibly well traveled and articulate, and my words are plain white cotton stuck to the roof of my mouth.

*My stories are interesting to some, but theatre experiences
hold little fascination for people outside of the business.*

*I've invited my dear friend Greg to come to dinner with
us, and I am so glad I did. Greg can talk to anyone and
he easily fills the gaps in conversation, giving me time to
take my brother in. They speak of travel and places they've
been, and I say I've been to Peoria, Illinois and they don't
get my joke. I'm not even sure I do. I try to be bubbly and
loquacious, but I am failing miserably.*

*Nevertheless, Lee looks at me like I am the most beau-
tiful thing he has ever seen. I am his lost talisman, the angel
and guardian and protector that he has been searching for.
He tells me how proud he is of my bravery for reaching
out to find my lost family, and I say, "It wasn't bravery." I
simply don't know any other way to love than openly and
messily. I had no choice but to find him.*

*I know that is not the case with everyone. I know some
people would say, "No, this life, this family that I know
is enough. I don't need to know the secrets. I am content
with where I am." But not me. I am NEVER content to be
where I am with what I know, so it seems the natural progression—the ONLY progression—reach out, bare my soul,
hope for the best.*

*Greg eases the tension and I watch the two of them con-
verse. They are comfortable with one another and I can tell
Greg genuinely likes Lee, so I am, for the moment, relieved.
When Greg leaves, the conversation will be awkward again,
but for now, we are on safe ground.*

*The ride home from the restaurant is full of stilted con-
versation, and when we get back to my house, I introduce
Lee to my daughters. Their eyes are wide at his strange*

*dress and mystical bearing, and they who are never silent
are utterly speechless. My girls are characteristically reserved around strangers, but this is something more. They
simply don't know how to handle their Nana's death and the
apparition-like presence of this beautiful mystery man, my
brother. They understand intuitively that he has changed—
will change—my life. Suddenly, this is very real to them too.
They have a Goth uncle, and he's standing right in front of
them in their own house.*

I am equally as bewildered.

*After the girls reluctantly head to bed, David, Lee and
I talk in the kitchen, the place where all good conversations
occur. Lee tells me again how brave I am and how grateful he is that I have found him. He applauds the work I've
done as the head of the Lost Sister Detective Agency, and
I wonder if he knows how much time I've actually spent
on the Internet, trying to discover anything about him. He
seems to have scrubbed any information about himself that
might have existed, and this bothers me. What is he hiding?*

*I talk about the emotional rollercoaster I've been on,
but I don't break down. I'm trying so hard to be cool, but
on the inside my stomach is quaking. Even though I feel
this intense connection, I am holding myself back from him.
I lean over the granite counter with my chin in my hands,
speaking of the depression I've felt since my mother's death
and my father's discovery. I don't make eye contact. Lee
asks gently, "Have you ever thought about killing yourself?"*

*My eyes jerk up to meet his. Why would he ask some-
thing like this? How could he know a secret I've never told
anyone? Could he intuit how dark my thoughts have been
these past two months?*

"Have you?" I fire back. I won't answer the question first, and certainly not in front of my husband.

"After my wife divorced me, I wanted to." he says softly. "I had the gun in my hand."

"What stopped you?" I ask him gently.

He looks at me pointedly. "I realized my life is not my own. It belongs to the people who love me."

I have these "dark moments of the soul," as they call them. The first time I thought about suicide was during my sophomore year in college. That horrible loneliness I have always felt overwhelmed me one night as I rode my yellow Schwinn back to my off-campus apartment.

I was still riding the bike I had won when I was twelve years old for drawing a picture of "Diggum the Frog" eating a bowl of Sugar Smacks whilst riding on a skateboard. Kellogg's, the cereal brand, had an annual nationwide contest called Stick Up for Breakfast, in which the best drawings featuring their cartoon characters, Tony the Tiger, Snap, Crackle, and Pop were awarded prizes. I was chosen as a first-place winner, and I got to pick out a ten-speed bike as a reward for my efforts.

On the morning I was to collect my prize, I ran downstairs excitedly and told my mom I was ready to go. She looked up from her newspaper bridge game and said, "Jim is taking you." My heart sank. Not only did I want my mother to witness my triumph in collecting my trophy bike, I did not want to be alone in the car with Jim for the forty-five-minute drive to the bicycle shop. I scooted as close to the passenger side door as I could, trying to put as much distance as possible between my stepfather and me. The ride was silent and uncomfortable, as usual. At the bike store, I picked out a cobalt blue three-speed with a glittery banana seat, but Jim curtly said it was too small for me and I needed something I could grow into. He pointed out the boring yellow Schwinn. Fine. I was sullen on the drive home.

That bike went with me to Michigan State University. My first day on campus, I rode it to explore the strange and unfamiliar new world I was in, and a frat boy shouted at me as I passed by, "Hey Freshman! Your ass is too fat for that bike!"

I refused to ride the Schwinn for the rest of the year unless it was absolutely necessary.

A week after the "fat ass" comment, I went to my first college party and lost my virginity to a sophomore with a thick Magnum P.I. mustache. I don't remember his name, but he later refused to date me because I was, in his eloquent words, good enough to fuck, but too fat to date.

Lovely.

I turned to dating men in the theatre department instead of frat boys, which came with its own set of frustrations. These men worshipped me, told me I was exquisite and all woman with my thick thighs and large breasts, but none of them would close the deal. I would sleep cuddled next to them, but no one was interested in having sex. What was wrong with me? Why wouldn't anyone love me?

I mean, my first clue should have been that they were in the theatre department. I had purchased a one-way ticket to Gayville. I believed that a man's refusal to sleep with me was due to my own ugliness and not his genetic desire for someone of his own sex. I was so naïve. I'm so grateful that those days of closeting and shame are swiftly becoming a thing of the past, but at the time, I had no understanding of my own sexuality, let alone anyone else's.

It was after the breakup of the third such ill-fated relationship when I was riding my hated Schwinn back to my apartment that I first felt the presence of the Dark Monster. I was sad. Overwhelmed. Depressed. I parked my bike in the rack and didn't lock it. I was hoping someone would steal it. I looked up at my building and stared at the roof four stories up. I could climb the stairs, walk to the edge and jump. I would not have to deal with the nightmares and the fat comments and the frustrated sexual feelings for men who would never love me. Just jump. Easy. Wouldn't everyone be better off if I was just gone?

But I couldn't do it. I sat by the bike rack and sobbed. I was both afraid to live and afraid to die.

There have been other times, deep depression-saturated moments, when I've had suicidal ideation. I dreamt of taking pills and just going to sleep; or driving the car over the median into oncoming traffic; or getting a gun and shoving it in my mouth and pulling the trigger; or bleeding out in the bathtub. I kept a razor blade hidden in my studio just in case I ever decided to slit my wrists. These sinkhole moments terrify me. I don't believe I would ever actually turn the wheel or pull the trigger, but even having the thoughts is terrifying. Dangerous. Warning signs. But these thoughts are my secret.

So, when in my kitchen Lee says his life is not his own, that he belongs to the people who love him, I know he understands exactly what I have been thinking. He wants me to know that he loves me and that my life now belongs to him. He knows what I have never told a single living soul.

That is how I know he is not only related, he is my family. We are connected in some way that is intangible and thrilling to us both.

I say it's time for bed, and overwhelmed with feeling for what we are going through together, we go to kiss each other goodnight and realize, horrified, as our lips almost touch, that we are siblings. We both quickly swerve, and he ends up kissing my eyeball instead and then we burst out in laughter. We dodged that awkward bullet.

The next two days are spent discovering one other. I've invited my brother Dale and his wife as well as my friends Jill, Greg and Joan over for dinner. I need my friends as a protective bubble around me. I don't know why I still feel so afraid of Lee. Is it the person he is that makes me nervous or everything that he represents? I am inexplicably drawn to him, and I am filled with admiration and envy for his sureness of self. I already love who he is, without question, but I wonder how much I am like him. How much of his father, our father, is in me too? The overabundance of raw emotion is exhausting and leaves me feeling vulnerable. I hate that I am putting Lee on trial by inviting this jury of my peers to dinner, but that is exactly what I'm doing.

But he knows it, and instead of shying away, he leans in. He sits to my right at the dinner table and regales the party with stories about OUR father. He holds my hand and speaks to everyone, but he is looking deeply into my eyes as he does so, claiming me. I can feel Dale and Stephanie's discomfort, and I wonder if Dale feels like he is losing his sister.

There is so much electricity flowing between us, it's

almost palpable. We are in our own little bubble. Lee oc-
casionally looks away to ask Dale about our childhood or
to answers questions being thrown at him. He tells stories
of his lovers and his travels around the world, of being
kidnapped by Bedouins and witnessing a shooting at a gay
pride parade in Budapest. I know they don't believe him.
They think he is lying about himself, and I feel him locking
back into me because I am his sister, and I will understand
the things they don't. And I do. It terrifies me because all
logic says this is too fantastical to be true, but I understand
him. He is my brother.

I feel guilty when I speak about "Tom" rather than
"Daddy." I do so simply for clarification because now when
I say "my father," no one is sure exactly who I am talking
about. I start to call him Tom/Dad instead, hoping that will
convey how much I still respected and loved him as a father,
even if he was not the sperm donor. I choke on the name
Don, but I'm not ready to call him Dad yet. What do I call
him? I'm still uncertain.

When dinner is over my friends and family leave, giving
me hugs and covert glances to say, "Be careful" because
they are afraid of this goth stranger, but when Joan hugs
me goodbye, she pulls me into the corner away from ev-
eryone else.

"He's wonderful!" Her eyes are shining, and I ask her
if she believes all the stories he has told. "Every single one.
He loves you." And that one reassuring comment amidst all
the skeptics gives me hope.

On the third day of Lee's visit, I finally have a break-
down. Covering the myriad of emotions I am experiencing
is getting to be too much. I wonder why on earth I agreed

*to go with him to Denver to visit OUR father's grave. I'm
scared. Going on a trip with a brother...a man... I hardly
know. It's too much. I cry in my room for an hour before we
leave, but then I put on my Big Girl pants and say to myself,
"Let's do this." Lee and I leave for the airport together, giddy,
nervous, and excited about this trip to Denver.*

*After nearly missing our flight because of a gate change,
running through O'Hare laughing hysterically, gathering
others who also missed the announcement, we eventually get
on the plane. After takeoff we share cabernet and intimacies
of our lives; lyrics I've written and pictures of his lovers
and friends. He reaches out to hold my hand and the indescribable happens: Our pulses are locked into rhythm—the
blood of our father pours from both our hearts in perfectly
synchronized beats. It's a strong and powerful moment, and
strangely, it makes me fully realize who he is. My brother.
My family. Child of my father, and someone I could have
cared for and nurtured and to whom I could have been a
big sister. It is a profound moment for me, feeling the loss
of a life I never knew and the promise of one yet to come.*

*We share a posh little house within the Denver city
limits. It's modern and spare, like Lee. I am cluttered and
messy, but our first trip together requires something elegant
and clean.*

*In the morning, we drive to the florist to pick up flow-
ers for the graves of Don and my grandparents, Ora and
Averil. That smacks me in the gut. I have grandparents I
never knew—or knew of. Grandparents who probably never
knew I existed. Would they have doted on me? Shared stories
with their friends about their granddaughter, the actress?*

Lee and I drive an hour north of Denver through farm-

land. The snowcapped Rockies tower gloriously to the west. We arrive at the cemetery and it's tiny, rural, and bordered by a pasture with cows on one side and a farmhouse on the other. I'm nervous, but we pick our way through the graves until we find the one that says Donald Garnett.

I expect to cry, to keen, but I am quiet and in awe. The body of my father lays six feet beneath me, and it is the closest I have been to him in nearly fifty years. It's an emotionally charged moment, but I also feel empty, mourning a man I do not remember. It isn't until Lee wraps his arms around me that I feel it, rising up from the frozen ground: blood, power, and heritage. My brother, the closest thing to my unremembered father, holds me and I feel it resonate deep in my heart. Family.

I am home.

That evening, Lee cooks dinner for me in our little posh pad kitchen, and as we are cleaning up the dishes, I say, "I wish I could hear our father's voice. Maybe it would trigger some memories about the trips we took together when I was

young. What did he sound like?"

Lee, who already looks so much like Don, starts blustering and speaking as his father used to do. "Well, Miss Cory, I'd probably tell you you're so close to remembering him that if it had been a snook it would have bit 'ya." Lee turns his head to the side, and I see a profile and a nose that is just like mine, but also just like Don's.

Something hits me deep inside. Some reservoir of the past cracked open a tiny bit, and it floods me with a memory of what it felt like when Don held me as a baby. Lee is channeling his father, and something in me recognizes it. I lean into my brother and start crying. It is so frustrating, being on the edge of a memory and not being able to fully access it. I am Don's child. He was my Daddy Don.

Lee and I get high that night because we're exhausted from all this high intensity emotion, and also because... well...it's Denver. Believe it or not, it's my first experience with weed because I have always been the good girl and the singer who carefully protects her voice. Well, this girl desperately needs to break free.

I'm nervous and I can't figure out the timing of lighting and inhaling. Lee looks at me like I am a complete idiot for not knowing how to smoke. He's determined to unlock me, to give me a life I should have had. The older sibling is supposed to corrupt the younger, so we are in some bizarre mirror world where the reverse is true.

We talk for hours on the couch. What would it have been like if we had grown up together? I tell him about my fractured childhood, and I know he feels helpless hearing about the poor little melancholy girl who always felt a sense of something missing. "You should have grown up

with us. Our house was always full of love." Yeah. Maybe
I should have.

Lee talks about his father's Irish Setters and about his
mother pouring a full bottle of Old Grand-Dad bourbon
whiskey onto Don's head and then handing him the business
card of a divorce lawyer. "It's either me or the booze." He
chose her. Lee speaks of growing up not understanding his
burgeoning sexuality as a young teenager. I tell him, "You
should have grown up with me as your big sister. I'd have
taught you all about women." He says, "Yeah. Maybe I
should have."

He asks me about my sexuality, about my thoughts on
monogamy and adultery, and I won't give him a straight
answer. Like my mother, I have things to erase.

Lee looks at me with his now familiar and keen glare,
and I know he sees right through my evasions.

The next evening, Lee comes back from the dispensary
with a lollipop. He hands it to me and smirks. "This will be
easier for you than the pipe."

I roll my eyes, embarrassed I'm such a square, and ask
how much of it I am supposed to eat. He tells me the entire
thing. We continue talking and I'm not feeling anything, so
I get through three quarters of the pop before we head to
dinner. I'm fine until we sit down at the table of the hip
vegan restaurant.

And then, the high hits me.

Hard.

I cannot speak. We are holding hands across the
table and staring intently into each other's eyes and the
words will not come. I'm staring and staring and cannot
speak and the room is swirling and when the food I do not

remember ordering comes I cannot eat it because it is the most disgusting thing in the world but oh my god look how beautiful my brother is and oh my god he is my brother and are people looking at me and do they know I am high and holy shit I do not do this. I am a good girl, and this is what being a Garnett has brought me to: wasted with my new-to-me brother in a vegan restaurant in Denver. Mile High City indeed.

I was probably still high when I got on the plane the next morning, but I sharply felt the separation from my brother. We were already so closely bonded. My blood is his blood, and we recognize ourselves and our father in each other. I was so grateful and ready for this gift.

CHAPTER FORTY-ONE

JUMP

I believe that there's a beginning to healing. You don't see it coming, but it springs up like the tiniest pale green sprout after taking root in your heart. You can be drenched in sorrow, and suddenly, for brief seconds in the midst of your sadness, you find yourself looking forward to tomorrow—to a new dawn, a new life free from the demons that have been haunting you.

Or at least, that is how I hope it will happen for me.

Maybe it is necessary for us to break down completely. To throw ourselves into an abyss so deep and dark that we may never find our way out again. We have to break down, cry, release all that has been making us fearful. We have to jump, take a leap of faith.

But I fucking hate heights.

CHAPTER FORTY-TWO

STEEL MAGNOLIAS

February 2018—Munster, Indiana

The first audition I had after my mother died was for a production of *Steel Magnolias* at Theatre at the Center in Munster, Indiana. The monologue I had to read was about the anger a mother feels after the death of her daughter. She cries, she screams, she laments. For me the trick in this audition wasn't *doing* the crying and screaming and lamenting, it was holding back from doing it. I knew if I opened that door to grief, I wouldn't be able to control what came pouring out.

But in the show itself, I had to open that door. I had to publicly mourn in front of 350 people each night.

I tend to get these roles: the crying wife who has lost her husband; the crying wife who cheats on her husband; the crying mother who is losing her daughter. I am always crying on stage. I can cry and belt a high C simultaneously. Maybe that's because I cry so easily in real life. And maybe that's because all my emotions are always so very close to the surface.

But doing a show where you cry and scream and lament is challenging. You never really feel the joy and the fun that the rest of the cast does because that weight hangs over you for the entire run. You know the emotional monologue is coming. You know that you have to access the worst memories and pain in order to do your character justice. It's cathartic, yes, but it's also emotionally exhausting.

And that's how it was with *Steel Magnolias*. It was a cast of six women...six of the most delightful women I have ever known. The show was pure joy, funny, and smart and these women were also funny and smart and, above all, kind. They listened to me talk endlessly of my mother's death and the subsequent revelations without judgment and with great compassion. We talked about everything in that dressing room; actresses usually do, but in this case there was never the kind of tension or micro-aggression that can exist in a room full of divas. There was only love and compassion, and for that I was extremely grateful.

But still, when it came time for the final scene of the play, the one where M'Lynn recounts the story of her daughter's hospitalization and the turning off of life support machines, I stood in the wings, sick to my stomach, willing the nausea to subside. Sometimes, in the moments before a pivotal scene, I recall things that upset me to draw the emotion to the surface, so that when I enter the scene, I am filled with the pain my character is feeling. I open the door a crack so that when it has to be blown wide open, I am ready. But everything with this scene hit too close to home: M'Lynn describes Shelby lying in a coma attached to a dialysis machine. She describes Shelby's husband and father leaving the room, just as Jim and Dale left when they were preparing Mama for her final departure. She talks of holding Shelby's hand as she passed and the gratitude for being present for both her birth and her death, just as I was for my mother's death and...well...MY birth, anyway. This role, this scene, wasn't acting. It was reliving. It was revisiting my mother's final moments five nights a week for six weeks. It was breaking down in front of strangers. Some nights when it just overwhelmed me, I'd think, "Oh great. Here is where I lose my mind onstage in front of everyone. Here is where I have my public nervous breakdown and the story goes into the oral history of Chicago theatre. Can you believe what happened to Cory...?"

But I survived it, and those lovely women pulled me back from my sorrow every night.

On the afternoon of the final performance I stood in the wings, waiting for my final entrance. The floor was painted to look like a concrete sidewalk, and there were swirls of tan paint on the surface to give it an illusion of depth. And every night when I stood there, waiting for my entrance cue, I would stare at the floor and see faces in the paint.

The human mind is an amazing thing. We need to make order out of chaos, and so we look for patterns, for things we recognize. It surprised me, however, how many recognizable patterns I could find in the seemingly random paint swirls on the floor of the theatre. I wondered if this was my mind categorizing random shapes, or if I was slowly going insane. I saw two eyes, a nose, and a mouth everywhere. Sometimes it was a jawline and an ear, sometimes two eyes and a swath of floppy hair. There was one spot in particular that I looked at every night because it looked just like my brother, Lee. The other faces were more abstract, but his was clear.

On the afternoon of the last performance, I stood looking at the paint-swirled floor, looking for faces, and it jumped out at me—a face I hadn't seen in the past five weeks. A woman's face in profile. A delicate nose and perfect lips and a jawline and an ear and even a hairline. And my heart raced because it looked like my mother. And then I noticed that next to that beautiful female face was another, partially obscured. A strong nose and jawline and darkened eye sockets. I gasped, because not only was that face so clear, it was also so clearly Daddy.

We find signs when we look for them. Was this a ghostly visitation from Ernie and Tom? Probably not. But that is what it felt like at that moment. My parents were with me, always. Lee was with me, always. Don was with me, always, even though I wasn't sure what his face would have looked like to me live and in person. We are not alone, ever. I walked out onto that stage and did my last monologue and had my last public breakdown and heard the sniffles and saw the tears of the cast and the members of the audience, reliving their own pains and sorrows through mine. We all shared the communion of love and loss together.

I love theatre. It breaks me, and it saves me.

CHAPTER FORTY-THREE

TIME

When I was young, I would constantly have nightmares about my mother dying. I would wake from these dreams inconsolable, shaking and crying. Her absence in my dream world was so palpable and real to me then. It was hard to shake the loneliness and the pain of the dream as I went through the morning. They were incredibly prescient, these dreams, because what I am feeling now—the loss, the loneliness, the utter despair—is exactly what it felt like when I was nine or ten, having these fearful subconscious reckonings.

Maybe time is not linear. What if those dreams were not just the fears of a child manifesting within the dream state? What if they were actual shadows of future memory?

There are many incongruent inconsistencies in time, things built hundreds of years before their alleged discovery: the Sphinx and its masonry construction completely out of time with the mud construction of the era in which it was supposedly created; the first written computer program by Ada Augusta King in 1843, one hundred years before the creation of a computer.

I'm not a scientist, but what if time and space is not linear at all but is happening all at once, and sometimes there is a crossover of events that allows us to peek through the veil of another time and place—a time and place wherein a child can experience the pain of her mother's death that she will experience forty years in the future. It's easy to suggest that as a child experiences the abstract loss of a father due to divorce or abandonment, the subconscious mind can turn it into loss of a mother to quantify it and make it something tangible, but I tell you, the loss in those dreams was exactly the loss I am feeling now. Except that, from this nightmare, I feel like I will never wake.

CHAPTER FORTY-FOUR

OF FAMILY TREES

After I returned from Denver, I became increasingly obsessed with discovering the life story of my birth father. My mother's friends are mostly gone, and while her sisters, Eileen and Joanne, knew about the affair, they didn't know anything about what kind of man Don Garnett was. Or at least if they did, they weren't talking.

Google could only tell me so much. I knew his birthdate, that he had a brother named Duane, and that he had a bachelor's degree from the University of Missouri and a masters in chemical engineering from the Illinois Institute of Technology.

I started scouring yearbook.com for photos of him in high school and college, and ancestry.com for newspaper articles. I built a family tree that went back generations, adding pictures of the graves of my ancestors to my online tree.

None of it made me feel better. In fact, it actually made me feel much worse.

What was the point of learning who these people were when they weren't really mine? I was never told the stories by my father or my grandparents. My grandmother and great-grandfather were still alive when I was born, and probably never even knew I existed. What did it matter to whom I was related or where their burial site was?

And then there was the other family tree, the Goodrich branch. I stared at the genealogy chart I had built on ancestry.com. All of the work I had done years before to find my relatives on Tom's side of the family was pointless. They were no longer my real family. Should I leave the tree intact? Delete it and build a new one? This tree felt like a lie. I felt like a lie.

In the winter of 2016, I'd purchased a pair of DNA test kits, one for me and one for my husband, as a Christmas gift. "I already know I'm half Irish and half French, why do I need this?" David grumbled. "Who knows, maybe you'll find a surprise." I countered. Secretly, I was curious about my own lineage (Hello, Intuition).

During the week before my mother's surgery, I logged on to ancestry.com to show her the results of my ethnicity test. Dale had purchased his own kit, but he had yet to spit in the tube.

"According to this, Mama, I've got Italian and German blood from your side, but I also have a large percentage of DNA from France, Ireland, Scotland, and Wales. That must be from Daddy's side. This also says I am Norwegian. That's odd, I thought Daddy was primarily English. But he was so tall and blond. He must have been Norse after all!"

Both Dale and my mother crowded closely around the computer.

"See, here is a section that will link you to other people who have done genetic testing. I can see who my cousins and second and third cousins are. It's pretty cool! Weird that

I don't really know who any of these people are, though."

I am so STUPID.

Of course I didn't know who they were. They were all from the Garnett side—the side that I knew nothing about. Had Dale completed his test before my mother died, we would have seen clearly that we were half, not full, siblings. I'm amazed he didn't do it sooner, but I think he may have been afraid of what the results would show.

I saw my mother scouring the report. She seemed to be taking more interest in my DNA results than I expected her to. Was she worried at that moment that I might be able to discover the truth? Did she think about telling me? Would she have denied the veracity of the test had I been clever enough to understand what the results were clearly telling me?

I will never know the answer to those questions.

So, in the spring of 2018, as I was busy researching my *new* family history, I was flummoxed about what to do with the Goodrich side of the family tree. I stared at the computer, tears welling up in my eyes. They are not mine anymore. In a fit of pique, I deleted the tree. I cut it down, just like Daddy had done with the mimosa trees.

I instantly regretted it, of course. Because as I looked at my new family tree, I realized that even though these people were blood relatives, they weren't mine either. I was neither Goodrich nor Garnett.

Then who the hell am I?

I tried seeing a grief counselor, but all I did was recount my story and cry as she frantically took notes to keep all the characters straight. Seriously, you need a flow chart. When I complained to her about how angry I was at the people who had kept the secret, she shook her head, bewildered.

"But they were protecting you. You shouldn't be angry at them."

I never went back. I didn't need more guilt. I needed a champion.

I was so depressed by this point. The suicidal thoughts were back, and it took all of my energy to keep myself from turning the car wheel off the road. I cried in the shower, in the car when "Journey to the Past" from Anastasia played on the Broadway satellite radio station. I cried when anyone mentioned family and when anyone didn't mention family. I was one big puffy eye bag. I cried at work, in the dressing room, onstage during sad songs. EVERYWHERE. I knew I was beginning to alarm (and annoy) my friends and family, but I couldn't help it. I couldn't hold anything back. I was a constant ball of AngerJoyGriefDespair. The past that I had no power to change was looming over me like a storm cloud, threatening to swallow me whole every second of every day.

I started telling my story to strangers, to check-out clerks, and to my seatmates on airplanes. Jim had asked me not to tell anyone about my mother's secret, and in rebellious response I told *everyone*. While seeing the incredulity on each stranger's face was validating and a little rewarding, it still left me feeling empty. I was in a bad state. I tried many forms of self-medication. Alcohol, Xanax, travel, yoga, baking, writing poetry, writing music, painting. Some things helped, some didn't. I was riding on a rickety wooden roller coaster without the safety bar.

Lee and I planned a brother/sister trip to Italy, and I was happy.

I came back home and I was sad.

I did a show in Saugatuck, Michigan, and I was happy!
I came back home and I was sad.

I drank my way through Thailand and Bali, and I was happy!

....I came back home and wanted to kill myself. Literally. Not metaphorically.

I was searching for anything that would lift this black cloud that surrounded me. I saw the world through a thick smog of weighty grey depression.

I can hear you out there saying, "For God's sake, get medication," and I heard that from everyone around me too. But I couldn't do it. For me, I knew it would only mask the pain.

I took antidepressants when my daughter Genevieve was born. I had horrible postpartum depression after Celia's birth, and in order to circumvent that happening again, my doctor prescribed Zoloft. I took the medication and it worked. I felt fine. Not great, not horrible, just fine. It wasn't until I was doing an emotional scene onstage that I realized I had lost all ability to connect with my darker emotions.

Gen was nine months old and I was playing Laurey in "Oklahoma". I was far too old to be playing an ingenue in love with a cocky cowboy but hey, a girl's gotta work. I loved the show and the role and especially the beautiful Rodgers and Hammerstein music. I loved that Laurey was a bit of a brat and was falling in love with Cowboy Curly, all the while grappling with her dark sexual attraction to Jud, the obsessively creepy farmhand who loved her.

Jud was played by my good friend Larry Adams. We'd worked together many times before and were comfortable together. There is a scene in which Laurey fears for her physical safety and eventually fires Jud. This scene should crackle with rage and fear. Onstage, I felt nothing. Every line I said was by the numbers. Cold. Fake. I could not work up a genuine tear to save my soul.

And in that moment, I realized *I'm an actress, I need access to my emotions, this is bullshit.* The next morning, I stopped taking the medication. Cold turkey. Ouch. Like my mother, when I decide I'm done with something, I'm done.

It was among the stupidest things I have ever done. I ended up sobbing for weeks. One day David came home from work and found me curled up in the fetal position on the kitchen floor, Gen in the bouncy chair and Celia coloring next to me. I couldn't move, all I could do was silently bleed. My serotonin levels were depleted without the drug. It's a bit of a miracle I made it through that sudden shock to my system. My doctor read me the riot act, and rightly so.

I worried that if I started taking antidepressants again after my mother's death and the subsequent revelations, I'd be on them for the rest of my life. I simply wasn't willing to do that again, to feel the soul sucking blandness of Zoloft or the whirling vortex of withdrawal.

Please understand, I am in NO WAY advocating that people don't take antidepressants if they need them. That would be a horribly irresponsible suggestion. In retrospect, given my history, I should have started taking them immediately after my mother died, but something held me back. I am very aware how lucky I am to have made it through my darkest moments.

I simply knew that I was going to have to feel every single second of this pain in all of its full, unadulterated, searing glory in order to come out whole on the other side.

I understood that I was on a spirit quest. The most intense spiritual journey of my life. It would either define me or break me. The only way past was through. No one will ever be able to accuse me of not facing the pain of my situation head on.

I don't have the answers for anyone else who is going through this sort of trauma...and it IS trauma. I can only tell you, as honestly as I can, how I handled things. Some decisions were good, others horrible, but they were my decisions, and I have to own them.

CHAPTER FORTY-FIVE

PENNIES FROM HEAVEN

February 2018

I snail mailed a letter to Dixie Garnett. I didn't have her email address, but even so, I probably wouldn't have used it. I wanted to do this old school, and a handwritten note seemed the proper way for an illegitimate child... *ahem*...love child to reach out to the woman who would have been her stepmother.

I was nervous because I couldn't predict how she would react, and also, if I'm being totally honest, if she even existed. Everything about Lee was so fantastical—his world travels, his stories about the woman shot through the ankle at a gay pride march, being kidnapped by Bedouins...maybe those stories were fantasy, and therefore maybe Dixie was fantasy too.

Ok, I know. There were marriage records and birth certificates and obviously Dixie really was Lee's mother, but my paranoia was in full swing at that point. Everything, from my mother's death to the subsequent revelations to the real-life appearance of my dream brother seemed too implausible to be true. Surely, I was in a Lifetime movie of the week.

So, to prove to myself that I wasn't, I sent the note.

I wasn't expecting a response quickly, so when a package was delivered to my doorstep only a week later, I was surprised.

I opened the box and read Dixie's letter. She was still deeply mourning the loss of her husband and refused to talk about him with me. She hoped I understood how painful it would be for her to do so. I was disappointed by this response. After all, I had so many questions. But as consolation, she sent along a few of my father's possessions that she felt I should have.

Even before I opened the enclosed pouches, I was shaking. These were personal items owned by my father. Things he cherished, possessions he had touched, and maybe they still contained his energy or essence. I am not normally so weirdly metaphysical, but since nothing is as it was, I suppose I have to allow myself some sentimental quirks and hippi-dippiness.

When I opened the first pouch, I started to weep.

My mother had a strange obsession with coins, silver and gold dollars specifically. Each of the OGs—the original four Goodrich children—inherited gold and silver coins from our mother. She had them wrapped in a metal enclosure and then had them made into pendants for necklaces or bracelets. I'm not exactly sure why, none of us has ever worn them, but maybe it was common practice in the '70s to wear this type of jewelry. It was always very synonymous with my memory of my mom.

So, when I opened the first pouch from Dixie and found

a silver coin transformed into a keychain, I knew instantly it was from my mother. It had to be. Who else would have done this?

Sure enough, Dixie shared the story of this cherished object. "When we first moved into our new house together, I saw Donald putting this keychain into the armoire, and I said, 'Ooo, I like that.' He told me it was a gift from Ernie."

It was all real.

This whole story has been, to me, conjectural. Other than the DNA test, where was the physical proof? Who was to say that this was a love affair and not a one-night stand? Where was the validation that I was conceived intentionally? How did I know my mother truly loved this man and he loved her? Or that he loved me? I had no significant memories of Don. I had no confirmation of facts from him, or from my mother, or from Tom/Dad. All of this could have been an elaborate conspiracy. A fairy tale. Maybe I was so grief stricken from the death of my mother that I had lapsed into insanity, and this was all a delusion of my diseased mind.

But a coin, a silver dollar on a keychain, made everything real for me.

There was a second coin also set on this keychain fob. A plain old ordinary nickel. What significance could that have, I wondered? I looked at the nickel's date. 1964. I was born in 1966. Could Ernie and Don have met in 1964, and did my mother memorialize that momentous year with a coin stamped with the date? It was so like her to do something like that. Well, to be fair, she actually memorialized the year with a coin *and* a child.

This keychain owned by my father and created by my mother was like those pennies scattered in the street—the ones found by my grief-stricken friends looking for signs sent by their loved ones from beyond. It was like the pennies, but it was a nickel and a silver dollar. Inflation, I suppose.

Signs. They pound me in the head, trying to get me to acknowledge them.

CHAPTER FORTY-SIX

ART THERAPY

Don Garnett was an artist as well as a chemical engineer, and one of his core beliefs was that everyone could learn to create art, or specifically, to paint. I've learned this from talking to my other new-to-me brother.

After waiting several months for my other two half siblings to contact me, I became impatient and emailed Michael. I was trying to give both of my siblings space, but there was just too much I needed to know, and let's face it, I am not known for having patience and reserve.

Michael answered my email, and we agreed to talk. When he called, I told him the whole story as I knew it. He was more reserved than Lee (he and Dale would get along famously). He asked me many questions, and I felt him trying to put the pieces of his past together.

He spoke of the difficulty of growing up with his/our father and said that his parents argued incessantly (I could relate). It was not a good marriage, even before beautiful Ernestine turned Don's world upside down. Michael had overheard arguments between his parents and suspected Don was "running around," and angrily confronted his father about his suspicions. Don was surprised that his son knew of the affair, but as I've said before, children are much more observant and intuitive than we give them credit for. I wondered how Michael was feeling at that moment, speaking with the byproduct of his father's "running around." Though he tried to conceal the pain in his voice, I got the impression that childhood was not easy for Michael or his sister, but despite the difficulties, Michael said he now tries to look at the positives. One of the biggest positives he received from his father was Don's artistic passion and talent. Even though the two were somewhat estranged in later years, Michael connects deeply with Don through art...

...which is odd, because I am doing the very same thing.

The winter after my mother's death I was desperate for some type of outlet for the overwhelming emotions that were battling it out in my head. I was no longer going to counseling, and I had talked my poor husband and daughters to death. Alcohol was numbing the pain, but I was positively bursting with an emotional energy that needed to be expressed. I usually poured my heart into song lyrics and music, but the words were stuck in my throat, refusing to come out.

The Dark Monster

One afternoon I picked up a pen and started sketching images since I was having no luck with words. I drew a cartoon panel depicting what my own personal depression felt like, a demon hovering over and around me, consuming me. When I finished that, I drew another series of cartoons depicting myself and Lee as the children we would have been growing up together. I was creating the life I never had. I thought, *aha!* This might be a productive way to work through my tempestuous state—art therapy. I went to Target and bought a cheap set of watercolors and a sketchbook. I started sketching everything that had any symbolic or personal meaning to me. I painted cardinals because they are representative of those who have died, poppies for the remembrance of loved ones, trees and mountains and mysterious figures hiding in the woods that were clearly my shadow man father in his beloved Colorado home. The cheap watercolors soon led to professional watercolors and acrylic paints (my father's preferred medium) and eventually oil paints.

I have my father's gift.

It blows my mind that not only can I paint, I'm pretty good at it.

I have never picked up a paintbrush in my life, and I believed that Susie was the artist, not me. I have never drawn more than a few outlined princesses for my daughters to color when they were little girls, and now I am a prolific artist. How is this even possible?

This is an example of the little things that I mourn, things that slap me in the face with their absence without warning. If I had known my father, would he have taught me how to paint when I was a child, the way he did with Lee and Michael? Would I have ever gone into theatre? Would I instead be sitting quietly at my easel, making pictures with colors instead of with my voice?

There's no way to know.

I remember my mother once asking me if I had ever thought of picking up painting as a hobby, and I said, "NO, I would be horrible. I have no patience or skill for painting."

And now, I realize the significance of her asking me this specific question, because of course she knew of my father's love of painting. They met in art class for God's sake. I'm sad that she will never know of my new artistic obsession, and that she will never know she was correct in trying to lead me in that direction.

And, I'm sad Don will never know how he has inspired me. He will never know that his daughter takes after him. Then again, maybe he does...

I connect with Don when I paint. I can't explain it, and it sounds kind of mumbo jumbo crazy, but when I sit in front of my easel, there are moments when I clearly feel my father doing the work. I'm not saying that he is a spirit jumping into my body and picking up the brush like the anxious-to-communicate spirits who *whoosh* into Whoopi Goldberg in the movie *Ghost*, but I feel him with me when I paint. Maybe it's my imagination. Maybe it's just the manifestation of my deep desire to know my father. But that doesn't matter.

I hold onto this feeling. I consciously invite him in. I sit with my canvas and say, "Ok, Don. What do you want to paint today?" And we begin. Is he really there? I suppose I will never know for sure.

One of my father's paintings...

...and one of mine. Coincidence?

CHAPTER FORTY-SEVEN

IS THERE WIFI IN HEAVEN?

April 2018

I'm back to wondering about the veracity of signs and conversations with the dead and whether or not they who have passed can hear us. The veil between worlds feels very thin right now.

What am I looking for in this whole epic search for the truth that would make me happy? Is there any piece of information I could find that would ease my sorrow? That would make everything better? Is there any point to digging for the truth when each piece of the story that is revealed only leaves me with more longing and emptiness? What is it that I need?

I've decided that I want proof that my father looked for me, wondered about me, Googled and checked out who I was. I don't know how I will find this information, but I know that I need it.

I walk the dog in the morning, and I am upset, seething at what has been taken from me. And that's what it feels like...

not a missed opportunity or happenstance, but something having been physically stolen from me. They—my mother, Jim, my siblings, Ivy, my aunts, my cousins, and the family dog—stole the chance for me to meet my father. By not telling me for fifty-one years that my father was alive, wanting to know me, probably still in love with my mother in some capacity, and therefore still in love with his daughter, they STOLE him from me. It may not be the truth, but that is the story that keeps me up at night. I'm angry and betrayed and abandoned and a billion other emotions that I can't even begin to articulate.

Why is it taking me so long to get over this?

Theoretically, anger isn't useful. It doesn't change the facts. It doesn't magically make my father appear or produce a Harry Potter-like time-turner so that I can go back and ask my mother the questions I should have been brave enough to ask. But I feel justifiable in my rage. I suppose I have to go through it, to walk through the full shit storm of emotions to come out on the other side with some semblance of peace.

Whenever I walk my sheltie, Sophie, in the morning, I usually talk to the holy triumvirate...My Father, My Mum, and Don's Ghost. Usually I say I forgive them, or I cry for their sadness, or I plead for help, but today, on this foggy morning in April, I'm pissed. I'm having none of that. Instead, I demand. I say, "I am not begging you, Don, I am DEMANDING that you give me a sign. If you looked for me, if you loved me, if there is a painting or a letter or some sign that you reached out to me, I want it. I am not asking. I am COMMANDING you to let that proof come to light."

I feel ridiculous making requests of dead people, but if

*nothing else, I get my anger off of my chest. For the moment.
I drive to rehearsal, still sad, still overwhelmed. And
during that rehearsal I receive an email from my half-brother,
Michael. I've been emailing him for the past few days, and
he sent me pictures and snippets of information about our
father. The two of them had very little contact over the past
thirty years, but he was trying to focus on the positives about
Don. I know I have stirred something up for him, and I am
truly sorry for that. It is hard for me to know that in trying
to ease my own pain, I may be causing pain for others.*

*I can't absorb this email from Michael while I am work-
ing, and, let's be honest, I shouldn't be checking my email
while I am onstage in rehearsal anyway, so I set my phone
aside until break. When I come back to read it, the email is
gone. It wasn't in my trash, nor was it in my current mailbox.
It had just disappeared. I do a search for "Garnett" and
find the email, and I notice there are a few other emails
in my search results. Below two other recent emails from
Michael is an email labelled "Donald Garnett on LinkedIn."
I'm confused because I don't even use LinkedIn, although I
had an account set up from years before. I click the email,
and up pops the subject line "LinkedIn Request to connect
from Donald Garnett." The email was dated January 24th,
2014. Four years ago.*

*I'm getting very used to vertigo as the world starts spin-
ning again. Here in front of me is a literal visitation from
the past. Why didn't I see this request four years ago? Why
didn't this email ever appear when I searched my mailbox
for anything from a "Garnett" immediately after I discovered the truth? I do know that I looked, just in case he had
tried to reach out to me, or bought one of my CDs, or was*

on my website mailing list. I checked emails and IndieGoGo contributions and Facebook friend requests, but there was nothing from a Don Garnett. Why did this appear now?

Because I asked? No. Because I demanded? I commanded he send me a sign. And he did.

I have no logical explanation for this. Maybe there is one, maybe there isn't. I don't care. I am taking this as my sign. I, who do not believe in signs. Skeptical me is now a believer, wholeheartedly and unabashedly. There are signs. It's impossible for me to believe otherwise.

CHAPTER FORTY-EIGHT

NPE

Dale's wife Stephanie alerted me to a secret social media group for people in my particular situation *(There's a "Your Mother Has Died and You Are Suddenly a Bastard" club?)*, thinking it might be beneficial for me. Though I know it is unfair, I was annoyed. No one in the family reached out to me to see how I am handling this mess. They dropped the bomb and then fled, hoping to avoid the shrapnel. Everyone has been blaming my mother both for the act of creating a child from an affair and for not telling me about it herself before she died. They talk in whispers. "Why didn't Ernie...", "Didn't she realize...", "She was a real...".

I can't make them understand why complaining about her "misdeeds" and labeling her as the cause for the divorce and subsequent implosion of our lives is actually more hurtful to me than helpful because they just don't want to hear it. Maybe they aren't ready to hear it because they have their own pain from her actions. But the bare bones truth is this: had my mother not fallen in love with Don while still married to Tom, I would *never have even been born*. In some

286 · CORY GOODRICH

twisted way, blaming and hating her means blaming and hating me for being a product of her "indiscretion."

I am afraid they do wish I had never been born. Often, I wish that too.

Despite my reluctance to take the suggestion of anyone who is not firmly on Team Ernie, I investigate this secret group. Why is there a need, I wonder? Because, along with the increased popularity of DNA testing from companies like Ancestry and 23&Me came an increase in surprises. Illegitimate children. NPEs.

The term NPE predates DNA testing and means *Non-Paternity Event*. It was used in genetic genealogy to describe an event in which the presumed biological father is not the actual DNA father. The term can also be used in the instance of an unexpected mother and is used interchangeably with *Non-Parental Event*. It was within this support group that the term *Not Parent Expected* was coined.

Let's say you and your family all get DNA testing kits for Christmas (believe me, I take quite a different view now of all those joyful holiday "discover your ancestry" commercials.) You take the test and wait anxiously for your results. But, when they arrive, in addition to your joy at discovering your unexpected Italian heritage, you also notice that while your mother is listed as a parent, your father is not. You notice all sorts of other unknown relatives who are now connected to you. You may even have a person or two listed as "close family" or a half sibling, and you have no clue who this person is. You have had a Non-Parental Event.

It takes a while for the reality to sink in. The test is wrong, I spit in the tube incorrectly. My mother shows up as family, why doesn't my dad? Oh.

DNA don't lie, baby. Did your mother step out? Were you a product of artificial insemination? Donor conception? Alien Abduction?

There are many possible explanations for the unexpected DNA surprise, and the discovery doesn't always go down easy for the child or for the parents and family who may have been keeping the secret. There is almost always fallout. So, a group of people all experiencing the same fallout, the same trauma and loss of identity and shock, is a godsend.

I joined the group, hoping to get insight into the emotional minefield of others in a similar situation, and I'm surprised and horrified and relieved to see that we are all on the same rickety roller coaster together. Most have had the always-present sense of "being different" from the rest of their family. Some share the same lack of trust in people, the same identity crisis upon the discovery of their NPE status. The stories vary, and the members of the group are in different stages of their grief and acceptance. It is an incredible relief to know that I am not alone, that others are going through these violent mood swings and obsessively researching their new family, only to feel both elation and depression from their discoveries. This is a club no one is eager to join. There is no secret handshake or special discount card for being a member. Instead, we get shame and lots of "but your father is still your father" comments from friends and family.

Yes, Daddy is my father, but he is not my biological father. I don't have his height or his nose. I have the Garnett nose. I look in the mirror now and THAT is all I see. I am a Frankenstein of family and DNA. Don is my Franken-Father, but he is not my Daddy. He was never given the chance to be my Daddy. Thank God for this support group who understands this nightmare in a way no one who hasn't been through it themselves ever could. I needed a soft place to land, and these similarly wounded souls all held out pillows.

FrankenCory

Some members of the group have been searching for their birth fathers for years with no success. Others have found their biological family and been rejected by them. Some are grateful they discovered who they really are; others are devastated. A large percentage of the members discovered their status while in their fifties (and older), and are mourning deceased fathers they never had a chance to meet. All are grateful to have a safe outlet for their sorrows.

Here's another thing we all share: We *hate* the term bastard. We're all on a mission, we NPEs, to destigmatize this term as well as "illegitimate." We are every bit as legitimate as our siblings, even though we were (sometimes) born outside of the bonds of marriage. We are weary of feeling like outsiders, less than.

Bastard is such a vile word. I see the shock on people's faces when I use it, but this is exactly how I feel, how this *word* makes me feel. Dirty. I have no reason to feel this way—I know my mother loved me. But I am the Dirty Little Secret. The Bastard.

This feeling is simply the unintended outcome of the lies and deception that went into keeping me from the truth, no matter how noble or out of protection the lies may have been told. But I am done with being a secret. I stand proud, and I refuse to accept shame or the whispers and gossip that accompany the talk of my conception. This was not my fault.

Let me repeat that, both for you and for myself because it is important: *This was not my fault.*

I did nothing to ask for this "bastard" status. Who I came from and the circumstances of my birth were not of my choosing. It is unbearable to feel the weight of judgement for something that, first of all, I believe is quite frankly the natural human condition, and second, was completely out of my control.

It is **conservatively** estimated that nearly ten percent of the population will find that they too are NPE's. Ten percent! And the number could be higher. Seriously, let that sink in for a minute. One in every ten people you meet could have a different father than they think they have. That's one hell of a chunk of people about to have epic identity crises.

There are a great many things this group of NPEs, would like the world to know. Most of us are not looking for our family because we want money or inheritance. We are looking because we want to know our own story. We deserve to know our truth. We're looking because we want our medical history. Are we at risk for heart disease, diabetes, cancer? We want to know where we come from, who we look like. We want a sense of connection—and wanting that doesn't mean we don't love and appreciate the family we grew up with.

We want you to know that a discovery like this is traumatic and we won't get over it in a couple of weeks. Or months. Or maybe, ever. And despite this knowledge, we will feel guilty and confused when we can't get over it in a couple of weeks. Or months. Or especially, ever.

We want you to know that these new family connections we are making are not replacing our original family. There is always room for more love.

We want you to know that we are often torn between the love we have for the father we grew up with and wanting to know about the father who gave us life. It sometimes feels like we are betraying that paternal love, and that feeling can put us in a very difficult emotional state, but we are compelled to continue searching because we feel the very strong pull of DNA.

We want you to know that pictures of our birth father and grandparents mean the world to us. We are searching for the past that we have been denied.

But most of all, we want you to remind us, when we are struggling with the obsession of tracking down our lineage, when we are overwhelmed with emotions of sadness and inexplicable loss, when we are feeling the shame of being kept in the dark like dirty little secrets, *we need you to remind us that we are loved. We can be whole again. We are a gift to those who love and need us.*

Another point that strikes me from the hours spent reading the stories of my fellow NPEs is that while many are devastated to discover that the fathers who raised them were not their biological fathers, even more damage resulted from the lies and cover-ups that followed their conception.

And yet, I wonder what other options did some of these mothers have? What choice did *my* mother have? Should she have run off with Don and left her three other children behind? Should Don have abandoned his wife and his own two children? Should my mother have put me up for adoption? Should I have been aborted?

There are a million different scenarios that could have occurred. I don't know what Ernie and Don and Tom were thinking in those days, but I'm certain the choices they made were difficult. Nobody was a winner. I'm not angry with my mother. I simply wish I could talk to her and ask her about the whys and hows of the choices they made.

But, as Mick Jagger so eloquently sings, you can't always get what you want.

Though maybe, if I try, I can figure out what it is that I *need*.

CHAPTER FORTY-NINE

SPRING

May 2018—Chicago

W*e see our lives through different filters. Sometimes they are rose-colored glasses, sometimes
they are BluBlockers.*

*I think about this as I hear the revisionist history of the
life and times of Jim and "Erni with an 'i'." Jim has come
to Chicago for a visit, ostensibly to drop off my mother's
china. He's driven for four days from Tucson to Chicago to
drop off the remnants of her existence. Papers and crystal
and silver. A life boiled down to objects; things that were
precious to her and are now, therefore, precious to me. What
is left of us when we are gone? Things? Memories? China
and birth certificates and divorce papers?*

*A strange thing happened moments after my mother's
death. A veil of resentment I have always felt towards Jim
somehow lifted. It was so visceral I could almost see it like
gauze. As her soul left her body that horrible afternoon, as
I held her hand and sang to her as she died, I could feel
something ascend—a small ball of light—and with it went*

this blanket of something indescribable that had covered us all. Maybe it was her feelings and resentment toward Jim, maybe it was her earthly cares and woes. Maybe it was just her life force that had enveloped us all—but suddenly, I felt compassion for Jim, because my mother was no longer there for me to protect. After her death, and for the first time since I have known him, I saw Jim crack. He was filled with regret. I have never seen tears or kindness from him, just yelling and sniping at my mother over things he wanted but couldn't have because of us.

But even though this veil has lifted, I am still uncomfortable and unsettled by having to adjust to this new understanding—and when he starts introducing me as his "special girl" to the neighbors who come to offer their condolences on Erni's death, I recoil. It feels wrong. I wonder if perhaps I am the one who has been unfairly influenced by my mother's resentment towards him. Maybe I am the one who is remembering things distortedly, looking through the wrong end of the lens. Maybe mine is the revisionist history.

During this visit to Chicago, Jim talks of the instant connection he and my mother shared. He met her at a time in his life when he hated women, all women. He refused to even speak to them, he said, because his wife had unexpectedly filed for divorce and he was filled with resentment and distrust towards them all. Despite his eschewing of the female sex, somehow, miraculously, he was still drawn to my mother's incandescent light. He sat with her in that bar, the bar where she often spent evenings with her girlfriends, and they talked. She confessed the story of Don and the child conceived in their passion. She laid out her secrets, but she never spoke ill of her husband, Tom.

And now Jim says to me, "She was unfaithful to Tom, how do I know if she was unfaithful to me?" and there is no mention of his own blame, his own participation in an affair with a married woman while he was also still married. He knows deep down that he bears some responsibility, but he can't say it, can't remember it, can't acknowledge his participation in ripping me from home and security, but I know he feels it because I intuit those dark feelings people hold secretly in their hearts.

He shakes his head in regret.

"I never told her she was beautiful. I was afraid if she knew just how beautiful she was, she would leave me. Why didn't I tell her?"

Oh my god.

My heart is breaking for his sadness, but I am even more devastated for my mother's. Yes. You should have told her. We should all say the things the people we love need to hear.

I can feel the overwhelming weight of his sadness, and I am forced to forgive him because at least now, I know he feels it. At least now I know he loved my mother.

On this visit to our house in Chicago, after my mother's death, Jim talks about the beginnings of their marriage, the difficult early years. He speaks of our moving to Clarkston, and he mentions that my mother begged him to bring Chris and Eddie to live with us, to be a blended family. She wanted to be a mother to them. The Brady Bunch.

But Jim refused. "I just couldn't see how that would work out."

Here was another one of those lightbulb moments. All these years I had believed my mom was selfish...that she had kept Jim away from his kids so that he could (inadequately) father us. But no, that wasn't the truth at all.

The truth was she wanted *the mess. She wanted family and to take on his children as well as her own. She wanted to love and be loved. And he refused to let her be a true partner in his life, a mother to his children, a part of his family. Distance. Again.*

Maybe this was the real moment she turned away from him, all those years ago. What would Ernie have become with a man who truly loved her, who could give her the unabashed love that she needed?

I feel sorry for them both, now.

The most interesting result of this critical analysis of their fractured relationship is that for me, a lifetime of resentment towards Jim is finally dissipating. This is exactly why I need to analyze our lives, to see them both as real people, not the archetypical Sad Mother and Mean Step-Monster. Because when I see their flaws and their weaknesses, their humanness, I can let go of the hurts they unintentionally bestowed upon me. I can release the burden I have carried—the protectiveness I felt for my mother and her broken heart. I can finally see Jim for what he is and was, as I see my mother as she was with him. I understand why she needed him. I understand why she couldn't tell me the truth. I understand that she needed an escape, someplace new for her illegitimate child, where gossip and prying eyes couldn't touch her or me. I begin to forgive. It's not easy and it's not necessary for Jim, perhaps, but it IS necessary for me.

And I am finally starting to see Jim for what he was; a man troubled with an inability to connect with his own family for reasons that run deep within him. Maybe it was the way he was raised, maybe it was the estrangement in his first marriage. But seeing his heartbreak for the loss of my mother and the desperation to finally reach out to his children this late in his life makes me realize that maybe I never saw the full picture. Maybe I only latched on to the parts that hurt and wounded me, and I was too self-absorbed to see the struggles of others.

The same feeling of forgiveness is starting to grow within me for my family, the ones who suspected or kept the secret. The ones to whom I have unfairly directed so much of my frustration and anger. How could Susie or Dale or even Jim have possibly told me the truth while my mother was alive, particularly when she, who was so strong and determined, would shut them down if they did? We all wanted to protect her. And they all wanted to protect me, no matter how misguided that decision has proved to be.

I have to let go. And I hope I am finally ready to do that.

CHAPTER FIFTY

PENDULUMS

February 2019

The Swing

How do you like to go up in a swing
Up in the air so blue?
Oh, I do think it the pleasantest thing
Ever a child can do!

Up in the air and over the wall
Till I can see so wide,
River and trees and cattle and all
Over the countryside

Till I look down on the garden green
Down on the roof so brown—
Up in the air I go flying again,
Up in the air and down!

—Robert Louis Stevenson

I t's the only description for the ride I am on; up, down, up, down, my stomach clutching at the top of the arc, waiting for that millisecond of weightlessness before I go plunging down again.

My mother used to read this poem to me when I was a young child. She would grab her big lavender-grey book of poetry and we'd snuggle on the chair by the window in her yellow bedroom. She smelled of Emeraude perfume and her hair was so soft. Soft like it was when it was as white as Gandalf's robes, lying untidily upon the hospital pillow the time I brushed it smooth with my daughter's pink plastic hairbrush the day before she died.

Grief comes and goes like the swing. One second I'm up, the next I'm down.

I was actually congratulating myself for having a couple of good weeks. No tears, only focusing on work, my family, and writing.

And then, out of nowhere, the anger rears its ugly head and slaps me right in the face and I am a puddle of tears with a side order of pissed. I never know what is going to trigger it.

This time, it's my mother's voice.

In 2009, Susie's oldest daughter, Heather, interviewed my mother to chronicle the history of her family. They were sitting at our breakfast room table, the same table where I'm sitting at this very moment. Jim was on the couch in the living room, listening to it all. Occasionally his voice popped in on the recording to fill in a detail my mother had forgotten.

Heather started by asking her Nana, my mother, to state her name.

"Ernestine Eslinger, last name Perkins. There were two other names in between but you don't need to know about those."

Erase.

"Do you have any fond memories of your childhood?"

"Memories, yes. Fond, no."

"Okay, Nana, do you have any stories about growing up with your two sisters, Eileen and Joanne?"

"Yes, but I'm not telling them."

Jesus, Mama.

She's like an armadillo with her impenetrable armor on the outside, curled up in a protective ball on the inside.

The interview went on for half an hour. Eventually, Erni opened up and talked about her mother's family and her father's, but she wouldn't say *anything* about raising her children, her marriages, her childhood. No emotions, no favorite memories, no happy holidays. If she did let something personal slip, it was negative—how much she hated the family trips to Atlantic City because of sunburn and sand getting in her bathing suit, how much she hated performing, how her mother kept her from school activities, how she hated the annual trips to Orlando to visit Tom's mother on her birthday.

She was relatively calm in this interview. Things are what they are, she used to say. But I was getting more and more upset as I listened.

I realized that, in the fifteen months since she died, I had been protecting her. Defending her. Being her champion. I had deflected the blame from her, made excuses for her being in love, even positively romanticized the whole affair. "I am the product of the greatest love story ever told!" I shouted. "She was protecting me! She didn't tell me because it was too painful for her!"

Bullshit, bullshit, bullshit.

She wasn't protecting me. She was protecting herself.

I knew this when I heard her voice on the recording, joking to avoid answering the questions and possibly revealing herself or her emotions. She was burying the past.

But here's the thing: My mother did not bury this story of my birth so deeply that the truth could never be discovered. She *wanted* me to find out about Don. If she hadn't wanted me to know the truth about my birth, she would never have left the clues like beacons of light for me to discover.

The two photographs.

The three letters.

The bracelet.

No, my mother wanted me to know, but she was too scared to tell me while she was alive. She wanted me to know, but she wasn't willing to be there to help me through it.

She was selfish.

When I hear this tape, I remember all the arguments we had when I was younger, the frustrations I felt at not being able to pry open the oyster shell of the woman who was supposed to have loved me the most. I suddenly feel the full force of all those nightmares I used to have of screaming and never being heard.

I think of all the opportunities she had to tell me...when I was so close to knowing. All she had to do was tip the scale: after Tom died; in the car talking about Liz coming to her house to beg my mother not to take her husband; the time when my daughter Celia was a baby and I said I thought she looked like Daddy and Mama snorted defiantly and said "NO.

She doesn't." The time I told her garnets were my favorite gemstone, and that I was strangely drawn to them. Garnets. Garnetts, for God's sake.

All these opportunities lost. No, not lost. DENIED.

I love hearing my mother's voice again on the taped interview. I miss my mother. I love my mother, fiercely, devotedly. But I am furious at her. I've been stuffing that anger down for fifteen months and now, suddenly, here it is. Loud and suffocating and all-consuming.

I packed up my things for work, threw my iPad in my bag, and headed out to the car, scowling and in a horrible, black mood. I heard faint music and I stopped, trying to figure out where it was coming from. Not from inside the house, not from the car radio. It was coming from my bag. From my locked iPad. What is the song that's playing? I recognized it...

Of course I recognized it.

It's "The Far Side Banks of Jordan." The song I sang as my mother died.

My mother knows I am angry at her. She can feel my rage from the afterlife. Okay, Mama. I hear you. Loud and clear.

CHAPTER FIFTY-ONE

THE VIEW FROM THE PASS

January 2019

J im asks me to fly out to visit him in Green Valley. He
wants to tie things up with his estate, to make things
easy on me when he goes, and he is lonely, ambling
about in the empty house he and my mother built together.
He needs to discuss whether or not to stay in the house or
move to La Posada, the elder care facility in Green Valley.

But there is also a third reason he wants me to visit.
Unbeknownst to me, David has written to all the members
of my family, begging for help. He is concerned about my
mental state and asks them to reach out to me, to help me
walk through this Lonely Valley of Grief. "She needs information about Don and your mother, and any specifics you
can remember are vital to her."

Tommy and Dale are silent, uncomfortable with sharing
the details, or maybe they just don't remember anything. I
imagine they must have repressed many memories of this
painful time in their childhood. Susie tries to recall what
she knows, and we are sorting through the detritus of our

time in Delaware, looking for patterns and clues about our parents' relationships and how that impacted us both.

I expect this connection and retrospective analysis from my siblings, but I don't expect it from Jim.

I'm ridiculously nervous before the trip. How could I be there alone with Jim for three days? Would we be able to maintain a conversation? I'm so conditioned to stay as far away from him as possible, how will we share three days in the same house without me jumping out of my skin, the way I always had my entire childhood?

But this time is different. I'm strangely calm. We talk easily. My resentment is gone. I can finally look at him as a human being and not as a Step Monster.

He needs to tell me his own stories—of growing up dirt poor in Detroit, of his time in the Navy and getting leave to fly back from Korea as his own father died of heart failure at forty-seven. He talks of his ex-wife, June, and their divorce, and how heartbroken he is about his fractured relationship with his own four children. He talks of my mother and how much he loved her, and how good she was to him in the beginning of their relationship; how much she had to put up with.

"We got married in August, bought a new house in Clarkston, moved you up there, and then I lost my job the next month. I took a new job for half the pay and twice the work. I was never home. I don't know how your mother put up with that. It would have been easier for her to stay married to Tom. I don't know why she chose me." Tears well up in his eyes. I have never heard these stories before. He has never shared them, and I was never willing to ask the questions before now.

"I'm a different person than I was then," he says. "I used to believe that there was a right way and a wrong way to do things, and my way was always right." Oh yes. How well I remember railing against that rigidness.

"It must have been hard for you and Dale, being ripped away from your father and your home in Delaware."

I sit motionless, unable to take a breath. He's apologizing for all the hurt he knows I carry, hurt that I've tried to conceal by not visiting, or not carrying on conversations, or not being in the same room with him. I never thought he saw it, but perhaps he did.

"What is going to keep you going, Jim? You need something to focus on now that Mama is gone, to give you a reason to live. Are you going to write your book? Take that trip to Vietnam? What do you want to do with the rest of your time? What is your purpose?"

"My purpose now is to help you."

Shit.

No, don't be nice to me now. Don't make me have to reconcile all these emotions I've carried for years. If you apologize now, am I going to have to write my own revisionist history of my past, just like Mama did? To curate my own memories so they tell the story as I want it told, not as it really was?

But I know it is time. I have to not only let go of my anger at Mama and Don and the rest of the family but I also have to release all of the pain and anger I hold toward Jim. My mother's husband. No, my stepfather. I actually do have three fathers now. Tom, Don, and Jim. I'm like Sophie from "Mamma Mia". Three Dads.

"What is it that you are missing, that would help you

get over this situation with Don?" he asks.

I keep saying that I need all the info, that I can deal with the truth, but I can't deal with not knowing what happened, how they met, why they separated. I've pieced together as much as I can, but I still feel lost.

"I don't know. I suppose the one thing I need is something I can never have. I want to talk to him. I want to go back in time and let him know that I know he was my father. I want to be of use to him, to Dixie, to Lee. I wasn't there when Daddy died, but I was here for Mama. I'll be here for you. I should have been there when Don died. And I can't ever change that."

"You are too soft for this world. How on earth have you survived?" I tense up. And then he looks up at me, realizing he's reverted back to old Jim. "I'm just teasing you. I can tease you now, can't I?"

"Sure." And he can, because now I know it isn't an attack. And because he knows it sounded like one.

I am too soft for this world. My heart bleeds for every hurt, for my mother's broken heart, for my father who died without my knowing I was his child, for Tom/Dad dying alone, and now for Jim in his broken end-of-life state.

I hurt, but I know that I am alive. I know that I was loved by my mother and by Tom and by Don and yes, even by Jim.

Maybe, that's enough.

CHAPTER FIFTY-TWO

LOVE CHILD

F orgiveness.

In the end, this all boils down to forgiveness.

I've spent so much of my life being angry. Angry at my parents for divorcing. Angry at Jim for not being in the right emotional state to raise a stepchild. Angry at Anita for ruining my self-esteem by telling me I wasn't pretty enough to be an actress. And now, angry at all the people surrounding my mother who knew her secret and kept it from me, causing me to miss the opportunity to know a father who undoubtedly would have loved me the way I always knew I needed to be loved.

And yes, angry at my mother.

It's all horse shit.

I can be as justified in my rage as I want, but in the end, the only person it hurts is me. Anger no longer serves me.

I've been doing some pretty intense yoga the past couple months, trying to find some way to end this crippling depression, and I often get insights during savasana, (meditation). You know, thoughts I need to work through or images of the past that come up, whether bidden or un-bidden. I often end up crying on my mat, but I know that giving myself this mindful time is allowing me space to work through all the muck.

One of the things that has been said to me repeatedly during this process is, *"You have to forgive your mom."* And I've thought, *Yeah, okay, I don't really need to forgive her...oddly enough, I'm not angry with her.* She's the one person I am not truly angry with. Disappointed with, yes. Sad for her. Hurt because she couldn't share the truth with me, absolutely. But I've always known that this was a burden that she carried. What untruths—and I choose to say "untruths" rather than "lies"—what untruths she told were born out of protection...for me, for herself, for her other children, for my father(s). She wasn't purposefully trying to hurt me by keeping this secret. She chose what she felt would be the easiest path—*for me.* She simply had no idea how soul crushing this revelation would be.

Regardless, I've tried to send forgiving vibes up to her, but one day during yoga, it occurred to me that I don't really need to forgive her. I need to *thank* her. Thank her for bearing the burdens she did, for giving up everything she had to protect me, for giving me life with a man she loved but couldn't be with. So, I did. I lay in meditation and I simply said, "Thank you, Mama."

And when I thanked her, I felt something release.

I'm not in any way saying that everything will be per-fect now. I still have my moments of shaking my fists at the Universe, and I still can sink quickly into I-can't-handle-my-life depression. But I do know that we either are who we are because of someone, or we are who we are in spite of

someone. I've always believed I became who I am in spite
of all these people and things who had hurt me.

It's not true.

I am who I am *because* of them: Because of their weaknesses and failings and need. Because of their flaws and
their strengths. And mostly, because of their love.

I am not a bastard. I am a love child. I am their child,
borne and shaped by their love.

CHAPTER FIFTY-THREE

SCATTERING DADDY

Summer 1991

Ayear and a half after Tom passed away, Tommy, Susie, Dale, and I finally reunited at the house in Delaware. Our mission: to distribute Daddy's ashes on the Hercules Country Club golf course, a place where he happily spent most every morning since retiring. Daddy practically lived on those rolling greens where he had won seven lifetime hole-in-one trophies, found countless lost balls in the rough, and given all of us golf and tennis lessons, whether we were willing or not. There was no more appropriate place to lay him to rest.

Scattering ashes on private property is generally not permitted, so we "neglected" to ask permission, lest we be given an emphatic refusal. Don't ask, don't tell.

One of his many friends—everyone loved Tom Goodrich—had donated a bench in his name, so it was our plan to walk to the golf course late at night and scatter covertly; naughty children sneaking out against their parents' orders. We took the box of ashes (always simultaneously bigger and smaller than one expects), a silver baby cup commemorating Tommy's birth, and four flashlights and headed to the course after the summer moon rose to light our way.

The bench was not on the seventeenth hole.

Nor was it on the sixteenth.

Nobody thought to double check the location in the light of day, and now we were stumbling blindly in the dark.

The four of us were hysterically laughing, wandering around under a full moon while carrying the remains of our father in a cardboard box, searching for his memorial bench. We cracked jokes about Daddy, about our lives at the Hercules Country Club, about growing up together. It wasn't sad. We were giddy, happy to be together again as adults, comforted by our connection to our family and with each other.

When we finally found the bench, we went silent. Nothing was funny anymore.

Tommy took a scoop of the ashes with the baby cup, said his silent goodbye, and scattered Daddy around the bench. Susie took the next scoop and did the same. Dale followed suit, and finally, so did I. We were all grateful it was dark, so that our tears remained private.

Realizing there were many more ashes—Daddy was a tall man—we repeated the solemn burial ritual. Tommy grabbed a cupful, said a prayer, and released the ashes, followed by Susie, Dale, and then me.

We hadn't even made a dent in the box of Daddy.

So, we did a third round of solitary scooping and praying and scattering, nervous that the grey circle around the bench would be noticeable to the morning golfers, and suddenly the giggles hit us. This was going to take all night. There were SO many ashes, and we only had the one cup. We looked at one another, moon glinting in our eyes, said okay...let's do this...and started reaching in with our bare hands. Put Daddy on the green, he could get there in one stroke. Put Daddy in the rough since he always found dozens of lost balls there on every outing. Don't put him in the sand trap; he'd be so angry to be in the hazard. We filled out a score card under his name with a "1" marked on every hole and left it on the bench.

It was sacrilegious, irreverent, and ultimately, healing. We distributed our father as a family unit. We were bound together by blood and ashes. Bone and dust. We turned towards home, emotional and exhausted but fulfilled. Strangely, this night became a sacred, favorite memory of my family.

The Burying Tree, painted by Cory G.

October 2019—Arizona

Twenty-eight years later, we are together to scatter ashes again, this time with the addition of Jim. We are releasing my mother in Madera Canyon in the Santa Rita Mountains.

This time, there is no unity, no feeling of being bound tightly together. We are each in our own bubble of grief and loss. I assume we will follow the same ritual we had with Tom, and I am looking forward to regaining that bonded feeling, the morbid jokes and dark humor, the sibling togetherness. I need to feel connected, the way we felt on the golf course with our father, the way I felt when I was a Goodrich, not a Garnett. When I belonged.

But Jim has other plans. He and Tommy have divided Mama's ashes into five separate bags—Ziploc bags, no less. It feels a bit disgraceful to see her white ashes (of course they are white) held by the same container that might have held her lunch on a similar hiking trip to the canyon.

We drive to the cabin we've rented. Jim declares we will each find our own place to distribute our baggie of ashes alone. I protest, remembering scattering Daddy and the unity we felt, but Jim insists. There will be no solidarity. There is no honoring what her children may want, there is only his demand. We must each face our goodbyes separately.

Perhaps Jim doesn't want anyone to see him break down. Emotion is not his language, even though we have all seen him shed tears from the loss of Erni, his companion for the last forty-five years. Perhaps he needs to be alone, but surely the four of us children could repeat our collective mourning...

But everyone heads off in different directions. Perhaps I am the only one who feels the need for communion.

Fine, I sulk. You want to do this alone? Do it alone. I have things to say to her too. Things none of you needs to hear.

I walk, solitary amongst the trees, listening to the water of a thinly trickling brook. I look for a place that calls to me, that says, "Cory, bury me here." When I come to a giant white-barked tree, I feel it. It is not a beautiful tree. It is cracked and broken, one limb destroyed completely and lying at an odd distorted angle. There is one brilliantly white trunk, and four smaller grey branches grow from its base. It is Mama and her four children. Here I will lay my mother's body down. Or my fifth of it, anyway.

My insides are trembling, like I've had too much coffee. I don't want to do this. When I've released her ashes to the earth, will she be finally and completely gone? Will I absolve her from the pain of her hidden truths? Will she become a spirit walker singing her silent song of praise in the whistling winds of the canyon? Have I forgiven her enough to let the last of her body go free?

Let me goooooo.

I hear you, Mama.

I scatter my Ziploc baggie full of Erni(e) underneath the white tree, and it suddenly dawns on me. This is an Arizona Sycamore tree, which is symbolic of growth, persistence, strength, and endurance. The very qualities that Ernie embodied. The sycamore is also known as the Tree of Life, just like the Tree of Life on the "family" charm she wore every day, the one I have now and keep in her memory.

I scatter Mama's ashes in a ring around the tree, and I don't feel a sense of release or freedom, but I no longer feel the abject despair that has been constantly in my peripheral vision, ever present and silent, like Death waiting patiently in the corner of Mama's bedroom.

*Growth. Persistence. Strength and Endurance. "This
is MY life, Cory," she said to me, and now I say it to her.
This is MY life, Mama. Thank you.*

There's a boat that is waiting to carry me o'er
Over the Wild Western Seas
And the love that I long for to captain the boat
Is the love I've been longing to see

Sail On, Ernie
Sail Upon the Waves
To the Bright shores of Heaven
Where you'll rest easy there in His arms
You'll rest easy safe in His arms.

Though the burdens of life sometimes carry me down
And I often don't know what to do,
I know I'll be happy when finally I'm
On the Far Banks of Jordan with you

And this boat that will carry me shelters my heart
And my sorrow and grief shall not hold
For the lighthouse that guides me to heavenly shores
Shines a light that is purer than gold

Sail On, Ernie
Sail Upon the Waves
To the Bright shores of Heaven
And I'll rest easy there in your arms
I'll rest easy, safe in your arms.

CHAPTER FIFTY-FOUR

WHAT I KNOW

D on and Ernie met in art class. She was a self-proclaimed frustrated artist with no talent, and he believed everyone could paint.

I don't know many details of their relationship. I may never know them, because the intimacies died with each of them; the secret love letters of their hearts unopened and buried, like the unopened letters of Fanny Brawne to John Keats. Even if I could share their story, I'm not sure that I should. "It's MY life, Cory," she'd say. Maybe she's right.

I know they were in love. I know that my mother wanted to make a child with Don, and he agreed, and so I was conceived. I am not a mistake, a bastard, a bar sinister, a whoreson, nor a by-blow. I am a love child, in the truest sense.

I know that Tom/Dad loved me enough to agree to support me and raise me, even though I was not his biological child. When people say to me, "Your dad is still your dad," I agree with them. If anything, this whole experience has made me appreciate the type of man he was even more.

I know that when Tom/Dad discovered the affair, that he reported it to Don's company, Dupont. The company's response was to give Don a choice: either end the affair or lose his job and never work as a chemical engineer again. Then, they transferred him to their Houston plant. So, Dupont was effectively the entity that ended the relationship. Not Don. Not my mother.

I know that, had Don not been transferred to Houston, he never would have met his spirited second wife, Dixie, and their son—my brother—would never have been born. I can sometimes wax rhapsodically about the "what if's"; every child of a separated couple fantasizes about their parents staying together. But I also know that, had my childhood story had a fairy tale ending, my adult story would not have had one. I'm working on that happy ending. It's a struggle every day, but I am working on it. And I know the plot twist somehow involves my other half—the goofy, dark angel/ brother that I've grown to love so well.

Lee and I decided to travel together to Italy, and when I say we "decided," I mean I invited myself, and he graciously agreed. Then I hemmed and hawed and refused to buy a plane ticket because I was secretly terrified. But eventually, I screwed my courage to the sticking place and jumped. We spent eleven beautiful days backpacking around the country, drunk most of the time and laughing all of the time. Tentative at first about our new relationship, we eventually fell into a familial comfort, laughing over stupid jokes that only siblings seem to find amusing. We spent eleven days reliving the childhood we were denied. We were like puppies, falling over each other and biting and fighting and wrestling with our pasts, and we came out the other side as confidantes, friends, brother and sister. I know his is a heart I will cherish to the end of my days, and his acceptance and love of the sibling he never knew he had but always wanted has filled the gaps in my shattered heart like gold Kintsugi mends the broken pieces of a Japanese vase, making the vase more valuable as a result.

We also travelled together to Thailand, and on this trip, we started quarrelling. Not bad arguments but little squabbles; getting annoyed with each other and teasing just enough to rub the wrong way. Like SIBLINGS do. It wasn't all hearts and oh my god you found me's. It was real. During one of these arguments, I was pissy as hell, probably having a panic attack. Lee wasn't feeling well, he was suffering through a painful and as yet undiagnosed case of shingles, and he wanted me to go off and explore Bangkok on my own, but I was scared. I didn't want to go through Bangkok alone. It terrified me. It felt like he was pushing me away, like he didn't want to be with me. All of my rejection and abandonment issues bubbled to the surface, and I stood in the middle of our rented apartment crying, slightly drunk, full of anxiety. I blamed him for pushing me away, for not understanding that I was scared as a woman to be alone in a very foreign country. I told him he didn't love me, had no empathy for my fear, and I selfishly laid into him—my poor sick brother—unintentionally blaming him for all of the hurts from my past. In the middle of my epic freak out, he grabbed me and held me. I fought. I wasn't in the mood to be all touchy feely, but he held on tightly and said, "Pop wouldn't have left you unless he had to. I'm not going to abandon you. I will never leave you."

I struggled out the embrace and smacked him in the stomach. "Why did you say that!"

He grabbed me again in an embrace. "I will never

leave you."

He repeated a third time: "I will never leave you, Cory."

Tears. I cried so many tears. I never even realized how much I was projecting my father's abandonment onto my brother—the man who looked and sounded like him, the man who was the embodiment of a father I could never have. I never realized how terrified I was to lose him too.

I am so lucky to have found him.

I paint almost daily now. What started out of idle curiosity to see if the artistic gifts of my father were genetic has become a passion and a mission. I'm finding my voice as an artist, as a poet, as a writer. I am unabashedly embracing my bohemian artist self because I am finally free. I am no longer bound by secrets and lies of my past. When there is no longer anything to hide, we are free to be gloriously, fully who we are. I'm ready to see who that person is. I'm ready to embrace the truth of who I am and from whence I came.

I will never get to meet this man who is my father. That will break my heart every day for the rest of my life. I will never hear his voice, ask for his advice, have him walk me down the aisle nor feel his arms around me, but I when I paint, he speaks through my brush. When I hug my brother, I feel the love my father had for me, or would have, I hope. When I look at his picture and see his nose and his kind eyes, when I hear my brother muttering under his breath the same way I do, the same way our father did, I know I am a part of something perfect, something beautiful created by the union of two unlucky lovers, destined never to be together. Ernie and Don.

They live on through me.

EPILOGUE

It's been three years since my mother died and I learned about Donald Garnett and my brother, Lee. In that time, I have travelled with Lee to Italy; to Thailand and Bali; to Spain; to Austin, Texas; and to Sedona, Arizona. We have a deep bond that is indescribable to us both. We needed each other growing up, and we both feel the compulsion to make up for forty-one years of lost time. He pushes me to be freer, and he gives me glimpses of the man that is our father. When I hear Lee's voice, I hear a faint echo of Don Garnett, and I have a vague memory of the man who held me and loved me when I was young.

I give Lee the truth that he is loved and accepted for all his glorious eccentricities. I can't go back in time and be a big sister when he needed me growing up, but I try and make up for lost time now. We have a built-in wiring, connecting our thoughts and emotions. It's pointless hiding anything from each other. I feel seen and known, and I think he feels the same. We smooth out each other's rough edges.

I'm forging a relationship with Dixie, Lee's mother, and she feeds me pieces of information about my father; that his favorite birthday treat was pumpkin pie, that she called him Baby Boy, and that he was kind and thoughtful, and he loved deeply. She tells me I was never forgotten and that I was always missed. I don't know if that is true, but I hope it to be. I look to her as the stepmother I wish I'd had.

I haven't met her yet in person, but her emails delight me, and I love her spirit and her kindness. I hope I am helping her through her own grief and mourning as much as she is helping me through mine.

I know that I love my biological father with a deep, unexplainable certainty. He is in me, in my DNA, and in my spirit. When I regret not knowing him, not remembering his eccentricities, his fatherly advice, his calm embrace, all I have to do is close my eyes and breathe. He is *there*. Inside of me. He always was. I just never realized it.

I've forgiven my family for holding this secret. I know in my heart that things were withheld to protect me, or more likely, to protect *her*. There's no changing the past. All I can do is work to build a better future, and the only way for me to do that is to not only forgive but also thank those who were involved.

I still struggle with depression and anxiety. I fight it every day, and some days it is overwhelming. But other days, I see the glorious patterns of the universe; how all things had to happen when they happened to make me who I am right at this moment. On a good day, I can say it is a beautiful thing. I'm working for more of these good days.

I don't know when I'll get off the roller coaster, or if I ever will. There will be days I am angry at my mother and days I will thank her. Maybe it's alright to do both.

There are certainly moments I wish I never discovered my mother's secret. I wish I could go back in time and not ask the questions about the photograph. I would have mourned my mother's passing, but I would never have gone through this crisis of identity. Tom would have remained my father, and I would have remained a Goodrich but...

...then I wouldn't have found my beautiful brother. I wouldn't have traveled the world with him. I would never have discovered I was a painter. I might never have fully appreciated not only who I truly am but how complex and rebellious and loving my mother was.

And then there is Jim. My stepfather. He is near the end of his journey here on earth, and he knows it. He is trying to reconcile and rewrite his past, and he needs me now. He needs to tell his stories and to know he made an impact. At first, it all felt so disorienting to finally be considered a daughter by him. But he is making amends. He acknowledges he is not the person he was when I was growing up, and while he doesn't say it, I know he is sorry. It's hard. I've fostered my anger toward him for forty-five years. Who am I without it?

This change in the relationship is also difficult because now, I might just miss him when he is gone. It was much easier to hold onto my resentment, because his death is going to be difficult if I have forgiven him. But I know I have to, so I'm doing my best to move on, to let go of the hurts that shaped me. In some ways, I think my mother had to die before he did so that we could get to a place of peace. She was never able to get me to accept him while she was alive. Maybe she's using her influence in the afterlife. Not that I believe in that...I don't think.

I also have this incredible pull to discover more about my real father. I look just like him. I have his temperament and his insomnia, his love of painting and his overly intense hatred of snakes.

Cory and Don, both around the age of 7

Jim asked me why I care so much about knowing who Don was, especially since my mother obviously wanted me to be a Goodrich, not a Garnett. The answer is, I want to know who he was because I want to know who I am. Who would I have been if I had been known and loved by my father? Would I have had that ever present sense of loss, looking for someone I never even knew existed but who was still so keenly missed?

I should have been able to say I loved him and that I appreciated his loving my mother enough to create me, to look to him to see my past and my future.

There's a part of me that very much longs to take the Garnett name, but I worry about discarding the Goodrich part of me, of denying the love of a man who was abandoned by his own father and consequently refused to abandon me. I am both Goodrich and Garnett.

So, for now, I'll just be Cory G_.
I'll learn how to fill in the blank.

SPECIAL THANKS

Thank you to my husband, David, and to my daughters, Celia and Genevieve, for listening to countless rants, drying endless tears during this fifteen-month period of mourning, and for surviving my epic mood swings. You are my greatest gifts and the reason I keep going.

To my childhood friend, Jill Sengstock, for helping to edit this jumble of emotions and turning it into something readable enough to send to my next formidable editor.

To Elizabeth Lyons, for being not only that formidable editor, but also my champion and yet another weird synchronistic sign from my father.

To Bari Baskin and Time Stops Photography, for being the "Team Cory" official photographer.

To Dixie, for making me laugh and for accepting me fully as her husband's child; to Lee, for always pushing me beyond barriers I've erected, for telling me I worry too much, and for being the person I never knew I needed.

To Thomas Popejoy Goodrich, for being my dad and for being a role model of compassion and kindness.

To Dale, for holding onto the name Don Garnett for fifty years. To Susie, for writing countless words, trying to patch the hole in my heart all while trying to heal the hole in her own. To Jim, for trying to protect my mother's wishes.

To Don, for loving my mother and giving me his artistic talent and his eccentric genius DNA, his passion, and his nose.

And mostly, thank you to Ernestine, my beautiful mother, who drove me nuts when she was alive (and I her) and is haunting me now that she's gone. I am profoundly grateful to have had such a badass rebel as a mom. Go Team Ernie!

Made in the USA
Coppell, TX
15 April 2022